GURUKUL DAYS

A Diary of 3 year
Vedanta and Sanskrit Residential Course

Ashwini Kumar Aggarwal

with inputs by
SADHVI HEMSWAROOPA

जय गुरुदेव

Title: Gurukul Days
Author: Ashwini Kumar Aggarwal

Printed and Published by
Devotees of Sri Sri Ravi Shankar Ashram
34 Sunny Enclave, Devigarh Road,
Patiala 147001, Punjab, India

https://advaita56.weebly.com/
The Art of Living Centre

https://www.artofliving.org/

1st January 2022 a crescent Moon glows in the SE sky, soothing,
calming, pacifying – unfolding a Stability that thrills and satisfies.
Krishna Paksha Chaturdashi, Pausha Masa, Shishir Ritu, Jyeshtha
Nakshatra, Vikram Samvat 2078 Ananda, Saka Era 1943 Plava

1st Edition January 2022

जय गुरुदेव

Dedication

H H Sri Sri Ravi Shankar
the Master of KARMA YOGA, DHYANA, JNANA, BHAKTI, BLISS

An offering at His Lotus feet

Blessing

There is that Natural Inquisitiveness, WANTING to KNOW.

Bhakti is not against Knowledge. Lord Krishna says, when there's devotion, it incorporates knowledge within itself.

KNOWLEDGE leads you to DEVOTION, and devotion in turn invokes wisdom from within you.

H H Sri Sri Ravi Shankar
Discourse on Bhagavad Gita 13th Chapter at Bangalore Ashram
13 to 15 Aug 2017

Prayer

ॐ
सरस्वति नमस्तुभ्यं
वरदे कामरूपिणि ।
विद्यारंभं करिष्यामि
सिद्धिर्भवतु मे सदा ॥

वाक्यकारं वररुचिं भाष्यकारं पतञ्जलिम् ।
पाणिनिं सूत्रकारञ्च प्रणतोऽस्मि मुनित्रयम् ॥

Table of Contents

Introduction

Gurukul is a sacred place, where intense devotion flowers at the lotus feet of the Master. A gurukul is one of the rare systems of education, still surviving in isolated places on planet earth, on the basis of the lineage of the ancient times, when school was more than classroom and extracurricular activity.

Schooling in a Gurukul focusses on personality, character, integrity and honesty. It is a complete system of upbringing a human being. Apart from reading, writing, arithmetic and the arts, a gurukul teaches: Patience, acceptance, building a community, collective social responsibility, and a vision for holistic living. A gurukul is a place which grows along with the pupils, both physically and spiritually. Activities like construction, gardening and landscaping, celebrating festivals, and doing liaison work between the various government bodies and institutions in society, are all covered here.

I was especially fortunate to have studied under Mataji Swamini Brahmaprakasananda, who has a wonderfully balanced temperament, broad vision, and sound grasp of Vedanta. Her knowledge and thoroughness in Sanskrit grammar is legendary. I am also thankful to have had superb colleagues. My stay and learning have helped me in becoming a stronger and better individual in every way. I wholeheartedly recommend this program to serious and committed citizens of society, who wish to evolve as compassionate and beautiful human beings.

The Sanskrit Alphabet

संस्कृत वर्णमाला

Sanskrit संस्कृत is written in the देवनागरी Devanagari script, whereas English is written in the Latin (Roman) script.

Conjunct letter संयुक्त अक्षर

क्ष , ज्ञ , श्र are not letters of the alphabet. Rather these are conjuncts that have become popular in writing.

The Sanskrit alphabet is written with or without a halant. Consonants cannot be uttered without a vowel. In teaching, consonants are supplied with vowel अ for uttering.

Here are the 56 letters of the Sanskrit Alphabet.

20 Vowels (ह्रस्व दीर्घ प्लुत short long hail)

अ आ अ३ इ ई इ३ उ ऊ उ३ ऋ ॠ ऋ३ ऌ ऌ३ ए ऐ ए३ ओ औ ओ३

34 Consonants (with halant the half-marker)

क्	ख्	ग्	घ्	ङ्
च्	छ्	ज्	झ्	ञ्
ट्	ठ्	ड्	ढ्	ण्
त्	थ्	द्	ध्	न्
प्	फ्	ब्	भ्	म्
य्	र्	ल्	व्	ळ्
श्	ष्	स्	ह्	स्

2 Ayogavahas (Anusvara, Visarga that appear during speaking)

अं   अः   (ardhavisarga अᴈ)

Pronunciation of Sanskrit Letters

उच्चारणम्

अ son	आ father	इ it	ई beat	उ full	ऊ pool
ऋ rhythm	ॠ marine	ऌ revelry	ॡ		
ए play	ऐ aisle	ओ go	औ loud		

अं Anusvara is pure nasal – close the lips – similar to म्

अः Visarga is Breath release like ह and preceding vowel sound

E.g. utter नमः as नमह , शान्तिः as शान्तिहि , विष्णुः as विष्णुहु ।

क seek	ख khan	ग get	घ loghut	ङ sing
च chunk	छ catchhim	ज jump	झ hedgehog	ञ bunch
ट true	ठ anthill	ड drum	ढ godhead	ण under
त tamil	थ thunder	द that	ध breathe	न nut
प put	फ fruit	ब bin	भ abhor	म much
य loyal	र red	ल luck	व vase	
श sure	ष shun	स so	hum ह	

Conjuncts – first utter the top part and then bottom one, e.g.

Bhagavad Gita 10.16 तिष्ठसि → ष्ठ = ष् ठ

Bhagavad Gita 10.23 शङ्करश्चास्मि → ङ्क = ङ् क , श्च = श् च

Specific Conjuncts ह् ण = ह्ण , ह् न = ह्न , ह् म = ह्म

Utter with emphasis on the chest.

2-1/2 Month Vedanta Course Jan-April 2013

5:45pm 14Apr2013 Baisakhi New Year day.

Opening Ceremony 3 Year Vedanta Course 15/7/13

12:01pm July 15th, 2013 Guru Poornima

Swamiji's Birthday Celebrations 15Aug2013

11:15am 15Aug2013. Separating Rose petals in Kitchen for decorations. And noon puja in the Temple.

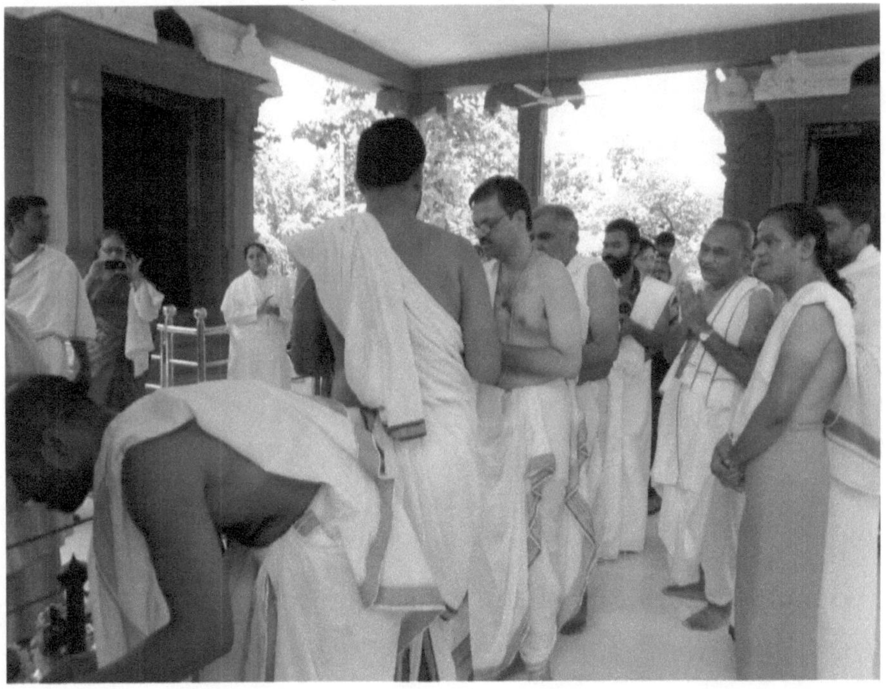

12:45pm 15Aug2013. Yashwantji sprinkling holy water – tirtham.

1:35pm 15Aug2013. Sumptuous meal in Kitchen.

Ram Tekri Visit 29Aug2013

11:24am 29Aug2013 Ramtek, Nagpur. A customary visit to this scenic spot. A story from the Ramayana retells Lord Rama's stay here. The famous Kavikulaguru Kalidas Sanskrit University is in Ramtek. https://kksu.org/

1:10pm 29Aug2013. Ram Tekri Temple

My Initiation into Sanskrit

In the Art of Living International Ashram at Bangalore, there was a National Conference on Sanskrit and Vedic Studies in February 2013. Mataji was also present, and I received Guruji's blessings and inspiration to go on this path.

Ajay, who at that time was managing the Art of Living Vidarbha Ashram, informed me of the upcoming Vedanta course at AVG Gurukul, and that became the entry point for me.

Earlier, we had done cursory study of Sanskrit in primary school, and I had the good fortune that my mother's aunt Shanti was an established authority on Sanskrit during my childhood days, who visited our home at times and spoke to us in Sanskrit.

As far as Sanskrit literature was concerned, we had all the Epics and Puranas at home, and we used to participate enthusiastically in the annual Ramlila festivities. Copies of the monthly magazine "Kalyan" of Gita Press Gorakhpur were also available at home.

My Day 1 at the Gurukul 7am 11Sep2013

I arrive in the wee hours of the morning at the Nagpur railway station, and board the waiting cab of a fellow named Narayan, who whisks me in a long arduous drive, and I step out into the dawn in a forest gurukul, where I am met by my friend Ajay, and escorted to my room No 14 on the far end of the first floor of the boys' quarters.

After a quick shower, we assemble at the Dakshinamurti temple, where there is a Rudra Puja happening. Then it is time to meet my new colleagues and exchange pleasantries, and finally I get introduced to Mataji, the resident chief acharya, who is our preceptor for the 3 year Vedanta and Sanskrit course.

Spending life in this fashion is a discipline of the highest order. It needs patience, acceptance, faith and hardwork. It needs the mind to be forgiving and helpful, and the body to be fit and functional. It is not easy, it is quite challenging, however it is hugely rewarding.

What follows is a photo essay that captures glimpses of life at the gurukul.

7:15am 11Sep2013 View from my room No 14 balcony of Boys Kutir that is East Facing and located in west of Gurukul area. To the right is visible the road that goes to the Academic block and further to Kitchen and then out of Gurukul. Far to the left is visible the two storey Girls Kutir located in north of Gurukul area.

4pm 14Sep2013. Cows arrived to graze. Adjacent Girls Kutir on far left is creamish Dakshinamurti Temple. Straight ahead is red Kitchen.

Gurukul Buildings Layout

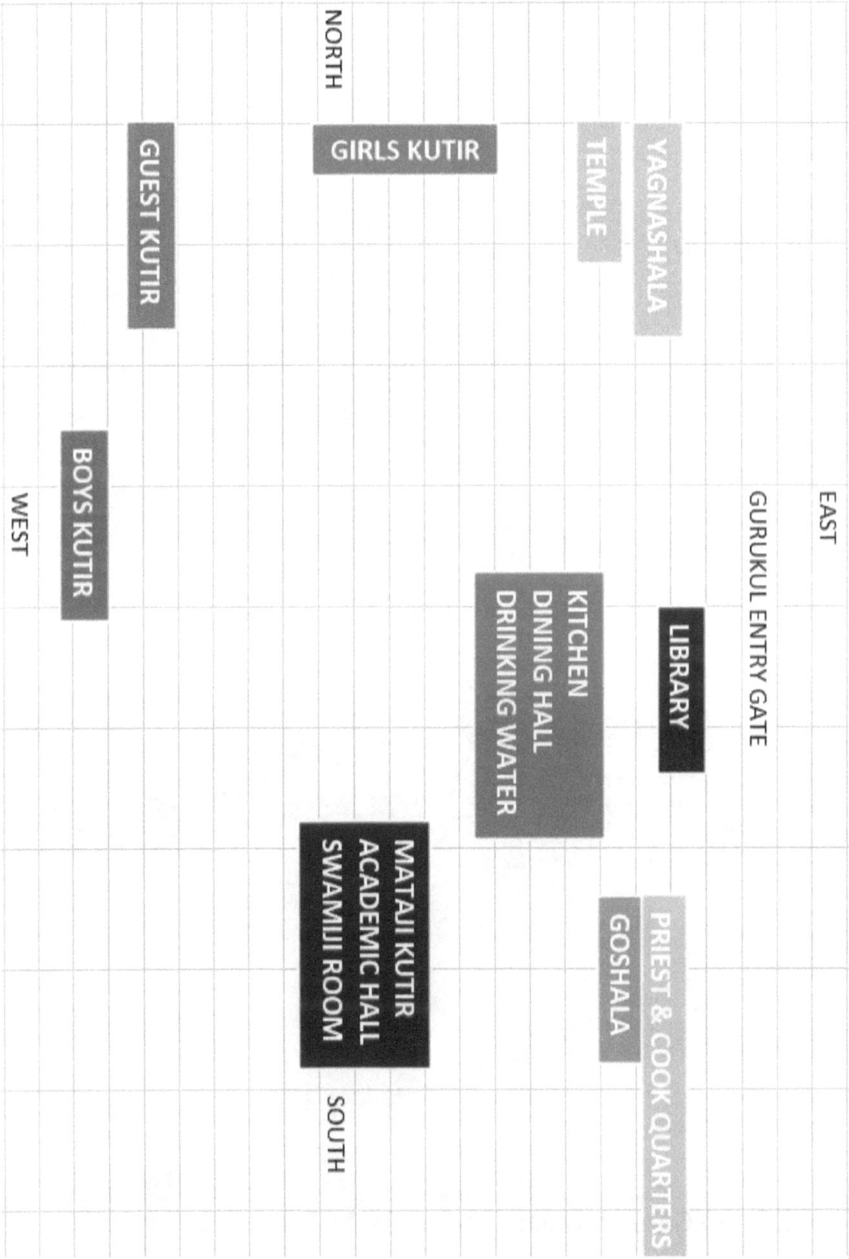

Gurukul Entry

Gurukul Entry Gate and road leading to the Temple at left. Office block is near the entrance far right.

Welcome board at 2km distance. T-junction at Dorli Bazargaon main Road.

6pm 24Sep2013. Ashwini and Sucheendra

A newly constructed house at 2Km T-junction Dorli Bazargaon road.

6pm 25Sep2013 Just entering the Gurukul, to the left we spot the Office building where Govindji sits, and it also houses the Library. In the distance to right is Kitchen.

View from the other side from inside the Gurukul, Kitchen in front and the upper storey of Library is visible behind.

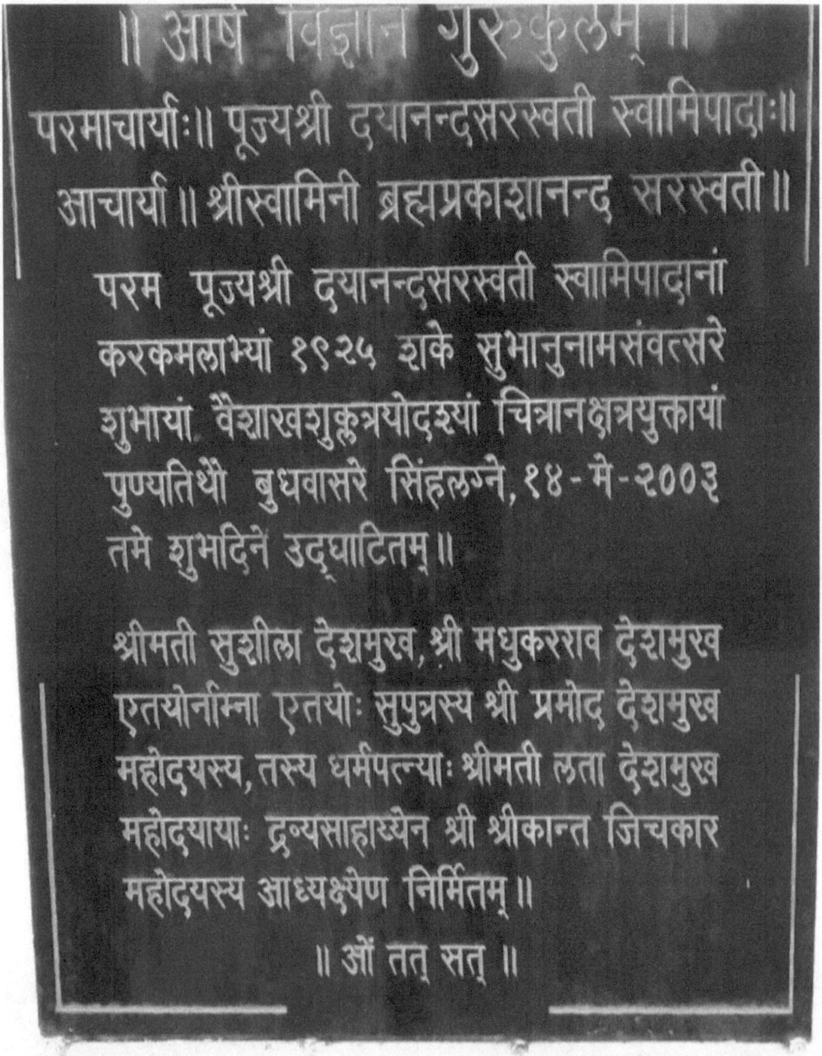

Gurukul foundation stone date 14 May 2003, installed at Office.

Girls Kutir

				First Floor				
ROOM 5		ROOM 6			ROOM 7		ROOM 8	
VACANT		ARUNA		STAIRS	SEETA		HEMSWAROOP	
ROOM 1		ROOM 2			ROOM 3		ROOM 4	
KRISHNA		LADY		STAIRS	MIKI		PRIYADARSHINI	
				Ground Floor				

10:46am 11Jul2013 Suma Nayak (mother of priest Subhash) at entrance to Girls Kutir. To far left is Kitchen, far right is Academic Hall.

10:50am 22Sep2013 Girls Kutir 1st Floor Corridor.

10:50am 22Sep2013 Girls Kutir Room 8.

10:26am 11Jul2013 Priest Subhash performing Puja inside room at Girls Kutir before beginning of course. Clockwise from center – sitting Yashwantji, Vinayji, Govindji, a Pandit, Suma in pink, Mataji, Shruti behind, cook's wife at doorway.

View of Girls Kutir from Academic Block. Temple is also seen.

3pm 14Dec2013. Some 50 yards behind the Girls Kutir is the crystal clear Stream where we do Puja and Initiation ceremonies.

Boys Kutir

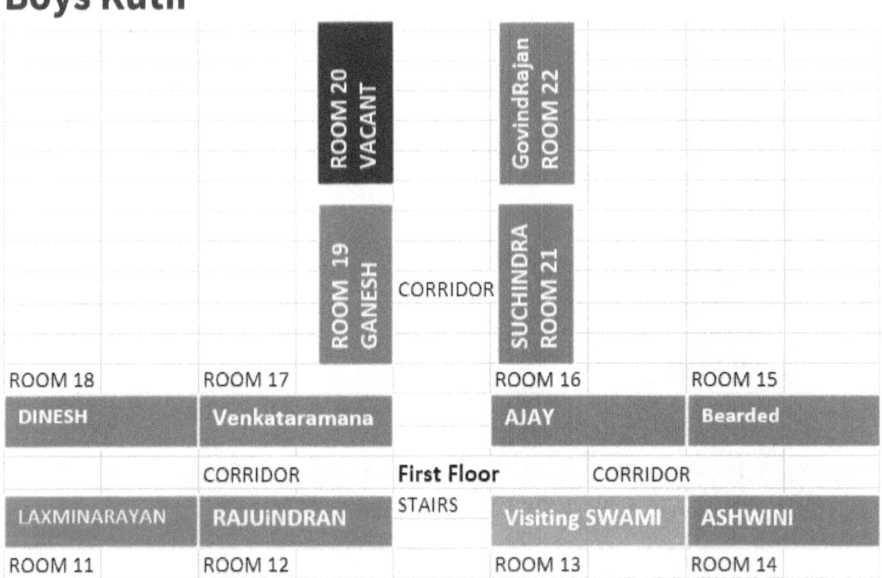

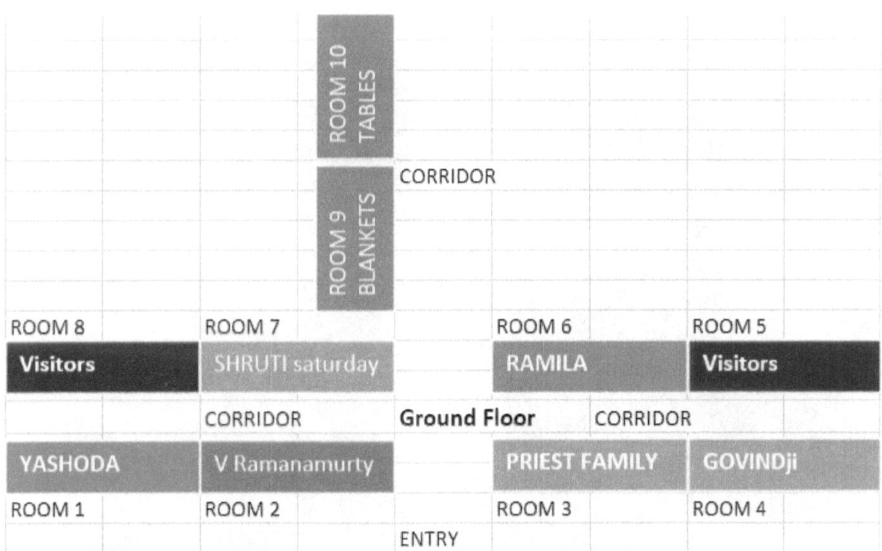

The Boys Kutir is located to the West of Gurukul. It is East facing and has independent rooms, each having an attached bath and balcony.

Boys Kutir flanked by Guest Kutir to right.

Gurukul Lake 1Km Long

6pm 24Sep2013 Lake at 2.5km distance from Gurukul.

6:17pm Waterfall stream from lake on Dorli Bazargaon road.

5:40pm 14Oct2013. Sunset at the Lake.

Lunch Time Prayer

We used to say Prayers before every meal. Particularly at lunch, Mataji ate with us, and the Dining Hall came alive to the benedictory formalities, which were customarily spoken in English.

Then one day, I translated the opening Prayer to Sanskrit, and from that day onwards, when it was my turn, I chanted the Prayer in Sanskrit to everyone's delight. Sucheendra followed it up too!

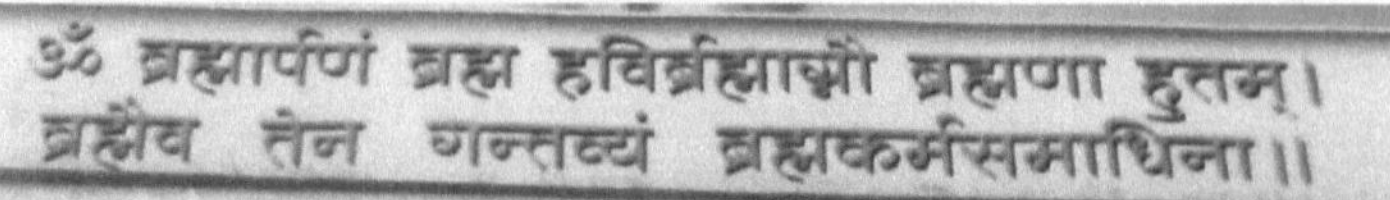

We chanted the entire 15th chapter of the Gita at lunch, and part of it during dinner.

Kitchen

1227pm noon 3Oct2013 Kitchen Dining Hall, open door goes out to Temple. The door in far center is cooking area, and steel table there is food serving counter. To right is chair on which Mataji sits for her meals. To left on floor is green seating asana for boys.

View from Mataji's chair. I sat in front of pillar from cold-storage. White Door at far end is North exit of dining hall, usually kept closed, it leads to the Temple.

Noon 15Aug2013. Birthday celebrations of Swami Dayananda Saraswati. Exiting from North door of kitchen and proceeding to temple, Ajay, Ganesh, Yashoda, Mataji.

View from Terrace of Girls Kutir. Red Kitchen, behind it is red Office+Library, cream Quarters for priest, cook, etc. Also seen is Water Tank and Gaushala shed.

Cook's family in the Kitchen corridor.

Daily Evening Walk

Almost all the pupils and Mataji used to spend an hour or so in the evening having a walk. Some of us walked within the gurukul premises, which was 500 yards rectangle in one round. Others walked from just outside the main gate till the Dorli Bazargaon road, a distance of 2Km. Sometimes we walked to the nearby orchards to pluck lemon, ber and guava.

Gurukul Cows

3pm 16Sep2013. Gurukul has a gaushala tended by the Vedic chanting acharya Yashwantji.

Saraswati Puja in Academic Hall

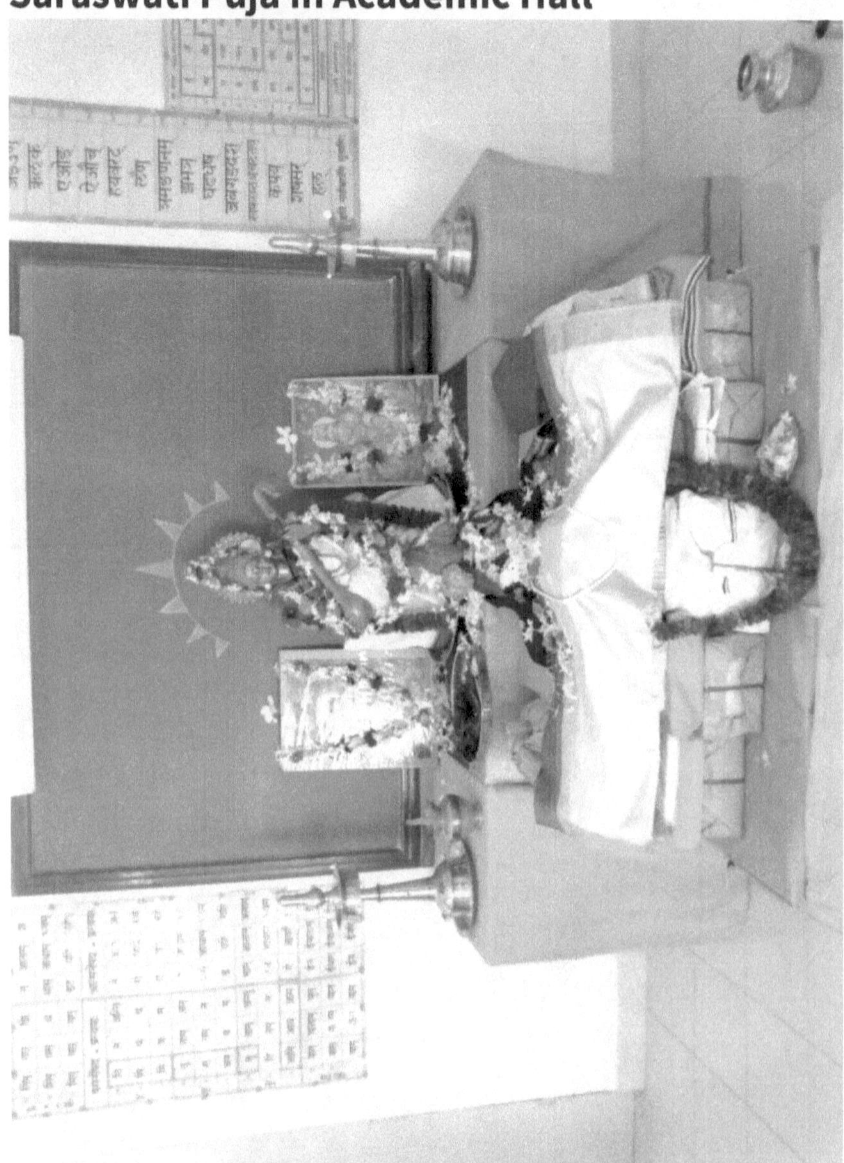

3:30pm 12Oct2013 Saraswati Puja for good education. We all chanted ॐ ऐं ह्रीं सरस्वत्यै नमः Om Aim Hrim Sarasvatyae Namah.

3pm 13Oct2013. Navaratri Navami Tithi. Our course books for dissemination to each pupil being blessed.

A year later same tithi.

Navratri Oct 2014

Academic Block

Entry steps to Academic Block. In the distance is visible Guest Kutir.

View of Academic Block from Terrace of Girls Kutir.

Road from Kitchen to Boys Hostel. On the right is Academic Block.

Car Parking

5:30pm 12Mar2015. Car park is on foothills next to Academic Block.

Left: Mataji's Bolero, Scorpio, Tempo for grocery/furniture.

Guest House

4:45pm 13Oct2013. Just to the left from my room balcony is the Guest Kutir located in NorthWest.

Dakshinamurti Temple

11:40am 21Sep2013 Dakshinamurti Temple located in NorthEast.

Temple idols are
Ganesha Shivalinga-with-Nandi Dakshinamurti Krishna

6pm 15Apr2015. Temple view from Girls Kutir terrace.

Temple Sthapati.

12:56pm 30Aug2013. Bhajan Sandhya at Temple. View shows temple entry gate and red office block in the far distance

Temple Parikrama, rear view.

7:50am 12May2007. Dakshinamurti.

Singing Bhajans

Our main singer was Ramila, who used to sing every evening in the temple during Aarti. Sucheendra had a good voice and he sang with fervor. I used to chip in occasionally by taking the lead, and everyone enjoyed joining in the chorus.

Abhisheka Water Buckets

We used to have Rudra Abhisheka every single day in the Temple. There were 3 large brass buckets that me and Ajay used to fill from the tap and give to the priest Subhash for doing the rituals. At that time I realized my fitness was quite good, as heaving those filled buckets was no ordinary task!

Saturday Long Walk ~ 25Km to Bazargaon

6:19am 19Oct2013. Going far walking on the weekend. Gurukul to Bazargaon was 12Km, and the to-and-fro walk easily made 25Km.

5:32pm 19Oct2013. Returning back, tired yet full.

19Oct2013. Milestone 4Km away from Gurukul. Bazargaon is a town bordering to the right and Dorli is the town bordering to the left.

Walking in the direction of Bazargaon, we climb a steep hillock. Ganesh Sucheendra Venkataramana.

Sunday Long Walk ~ 20Km to Dorli

8am 15Dec2013. Rich alluvial soil as we pass a farm, and a budding cotton field.

9:30am 10Nov2013. Venkataramana Ganesh Sucheendra, a break after a grueling walk. Gurukul to Dorli was 9Km, and the to-and-fro walk easily made 20Km.

Walking Chart of November 2013

Date		km	step	Total step	kcal	min	Stride Setting cnt
Sun	17-11-13	15.35	25772	36134	860.8	214	61
Sat	16-11-13	3-19	5247		179-2	47	61
Fri	15-11-13	3-45	5677		193-9	53	61

Orchard Visit 11/11/2013

3pm 11Nov2013 Ajay Rajuindran Ganesh Laxminarayan. At the Oranges Orchard for plucking and eating.

Sucheendra and Ganesh.

Govindrajan decides to climb and pluck.

A village home at the Orchard.

Back Row - Aruna Seeta Priya Ramila.
Front Row -Yashoda Laxminarayan Mataji Hemswaroop.

Cowherd befriended

During our evening walk, just past the bomb factory at 4Km distance from gurukul was a goshala. The cowherd and me became good friends, and I used to get a glass of fresh milk every time I visited. His father was a local saint of high order.

9:30am 9Nov2014 Mahadev the gorakshan (cowherd).

Gurukul Auto Service

Sanjay, our Auto Service guy from nearby village.

Prasthana Treya & Sanskrit Grammar Study

We used to have a packed schedule Monday to Friday. e.g.

4:30-5am Yoga and Stretching.

5am Rudra Abhisheka at Temple.

6am Prasadam.

6:30-7:30am Vedanta Prakaran Granth class, e.g. Tattvabodha.

7:30-7:50am Meditation.

8-8:30am Chants at Temple.

8:30-8:45am Breakfast.

9:15am-10:15am Sanskrit Grammar class.

10:15-11:15am Personal time break.

11:15-12:15pm Upanishad Bhashya Vedanta class.

12:30-1pm Lunchtime at Kitchen with group prayer.

1-2:30pm Personal time, siesta, etc.

2:30-3:30pm Sanskrit Grammar revision in Classroom.

3:30-4:15pm Playing of Ramayana Serial, TV time.

4:30-5:30pm Bhagavad Gita Bhashya Vedanta class.

5:30-6:30pm Evening Walk.

6:30-7:30pm Puja, Aarti, Bhajan singing at Temple.

8-8:30pm Dinner at Kitchen.

8:30-9:15pm Satsang, QnA with Mataji.

Saturdays were occupied from 10:30am to 2:30pm with Shruti taking Sanskrit Grammar revision and Bhagavad Gita chanting. Sunday was our weekly off.

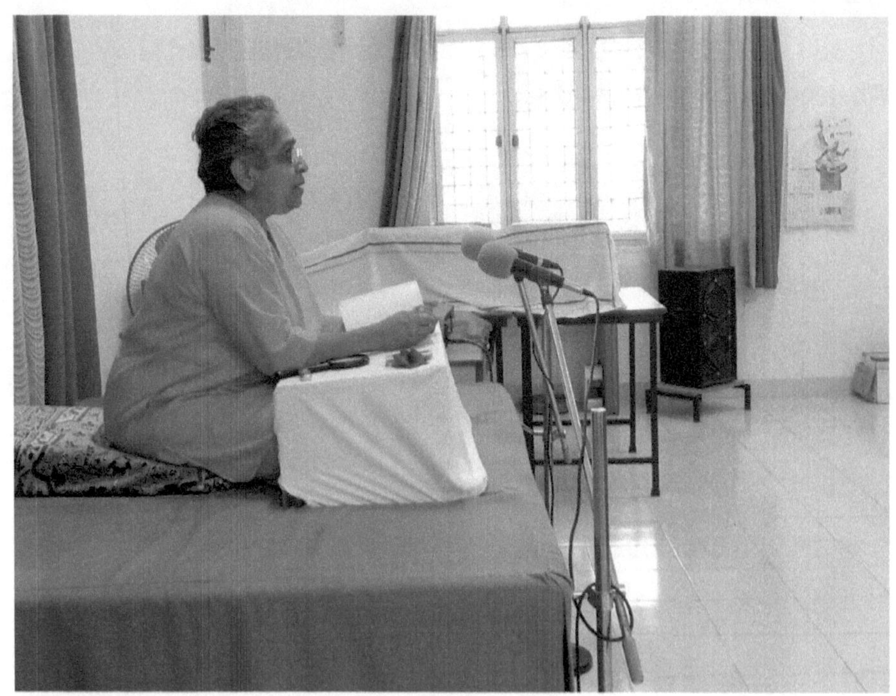

3:35pm 8Mar2014. Mataji taking Upanishad class.

9:50am 15Apr2016. Chanting Mantras in Class.

3pm 30Mar2015. Gerund Verb forms गम् + त्वा = गत्वा = Having gone.

4pm 13Apr2015. Dhatu द्विष् + तिप् = द्वेष्टि Present Tense Derivation.

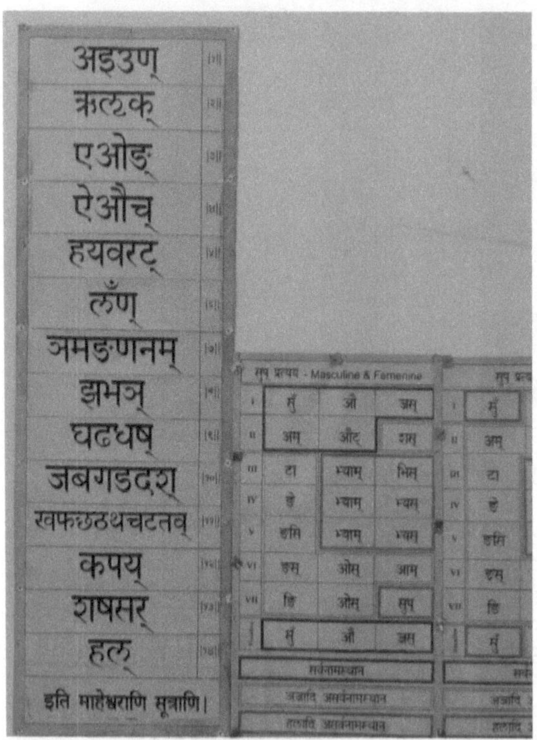

Sanskrit Posters in Academic Hall.

A Vedanta class underway.

॥ ९ अ.॥ काचिद् अन्तर्मुखा वृत्ति: पुण्यभोगे आनन्दप्रतिबिम्बभाक् (वस्ति)।
(सा) भोगशान्तौ निद्रारूपेण लीयते ॥
१०.आ॥ अयम् आनन्दमय: अपि कादाचित्कत्वत: आत्मा न स्याद्।
य: बिम्बभूत: आनन्द: असौ आत्मा सर्वदा स्थित: ॥

These two verses together describe आनन्दमयकोश & do the विवेक between आनन्दमय & आत्मा ।

Verse no. 9 defines आनन्दमयकोश । It says, this आनन्दमयकोश is a वृत्ति, which is turned inside, away from विज्ञानमय also & resolves in आत्मचैतन्य । From विज्ञानमय, everything upto आनन्दमय is external to this. When one enjoys a moment of happiness due to पुण्य, this आनन्दमयवृत्ति reflects the आनन्दस्वरूप of the आत्मा in itself. Whenever, the भोग of सुखाद:खंs for the day are over, this आनन्दमय resolves in the form of sleep. It resolves into आत्मा but the अन्त:करण is covered with ignorance. Therefore, it is slee
→(contd)

Blackboard written by Priyadarshini. Vedanta Class on Pancadashi.

Textbooks and Workbooks

I was fortunate to have a solid study group at Gurukul.
Venkataramana spent enough time with me in discussing the basic
concepts of Sanskrit grammar. Me Rajuindran, Ganesh and Venkat
devoted time to a regular sitting of revising the material covered in
Mataji's lectures.

9am 5Feb2016. Aruna receiving Brahmasutra bhashya textbook of
Kailash Ashram Rishikesh, from Mataji.

We studied using textbooks of Gita Press Gorakhpur and Kailash
Ashram Rishikesh, viz. the principal Upanishads with Adi
Shankaracharya's commentary and Bhagavad Gita Bhashya, in
Sanskrit and Hindi.

We also had temple chanting books from AVG Anaikatti.

For Sanskrit Grammar, we used Prathamavritti of Brahmadutt
Jignasu, Ashtadhyayi of Panini by S C Vasu, and Laghu Siddhanta
Kaumudi's Bhaimi Vyakhya. Many grammar books of Pushpa
Dikshit and Samskrita Bharati were also used.

Library Inauguration

All the pupils and Mataji worked hard to set up the Library, by shifting all the books from her quarters to the Office Block. The girls did the work of creating the ledgers and catalogs and entering each book by Subject and Author.

The boys arranged them on the newly procured shelves. It was a week's solid effort.

The first book I got issued was Amritsariya Ram Bhanot's masterly grammatical analysis of the Bhagavad Gita in 4 volumes. Much later I visited his home near Jalandhar in Punjab, and got the set of original books from his family, much to my erudition!

I also gave a set to Hemswaroop, and sent a set to Ganesh.

Learning Music Raaga

The esteemed Veena exponent, K. Subramanian visited the gurukul to introduce us to the nuances of musical notes.

3/10/2013
Music Class

9:00 pm Thursday.   Dr Karaikudi Subramanian

Gurur Brahma

Scale

M	P	D	S'	D	P	M	P
D	M	G	r	S	S	S	S

S	R	M	m	R	M	P	P	
M	P	D	r	S	S	S	S	S	S

		Svaras	Svara Sthanas	
	13	S'	Throat	
	12	N		
	11	n		
one	10	N	D	in a straight line with armpit
full	9	n	d	
octave	8	D	P	heart (sternum)
=	7	d	M	
The	6	P	m	below the breast line
Middle	5	M	G	
octave	4	m	g	
	3	R	R	
	2	r	r	
	1	S	S	Manipura

Krishnāya Vasudeyāya Devaki Nandnāya ३
Nanda Gop kumarāya Govindāya Namo Namah

6.10.2013 5pm

The G-sharp scale was given for practise.
pitch.

r ___________________   Practise saying आ

s ___________________   Begin from Navel

n ___________________

Mela Chart m

	S	r	R	g	G	m		P	d	D	n	N	S
1.	S	r	R	g	G	m		P	d	D	n	N	S
2.	S	r		g		m		P	d				S
3.	S	r			G	m		P	d				S
4.	S		R	g		m		P		D	n		S
5.	S					m		P					S
6.	S					m		P					S

The 4th scale above

S   R   g   m   P   D   n   S

is the Vedic scale (in vedic chantings)

Mela chart M

	S	r	R	g	G	M		P	d	D	n	N	S
1	S	r	R	g	G	M		P	d	D	n	N	S
2	S	r				M		P					S
3	S	r				M		P					S
4	S					M		P					S
5	S					M		P					S
6	S					M		P					S

The above Mela chart m, has 6×6=36
scale combinations. Similarly the
Mela chart M has 6×6=36 scale combinations

So there are 72 basic frame works
        ie 72 basic scales
        ie 72 gamaka movements

Gurukul Colleagues and Staff

Dinesh
Seeta
Govindji
Hemswaroop

Sucheendra
Ganesh
Venkataramana
Ajay

| Rajuindran | Mataji's Driver Moray |
| Yashoda | Ashwini |

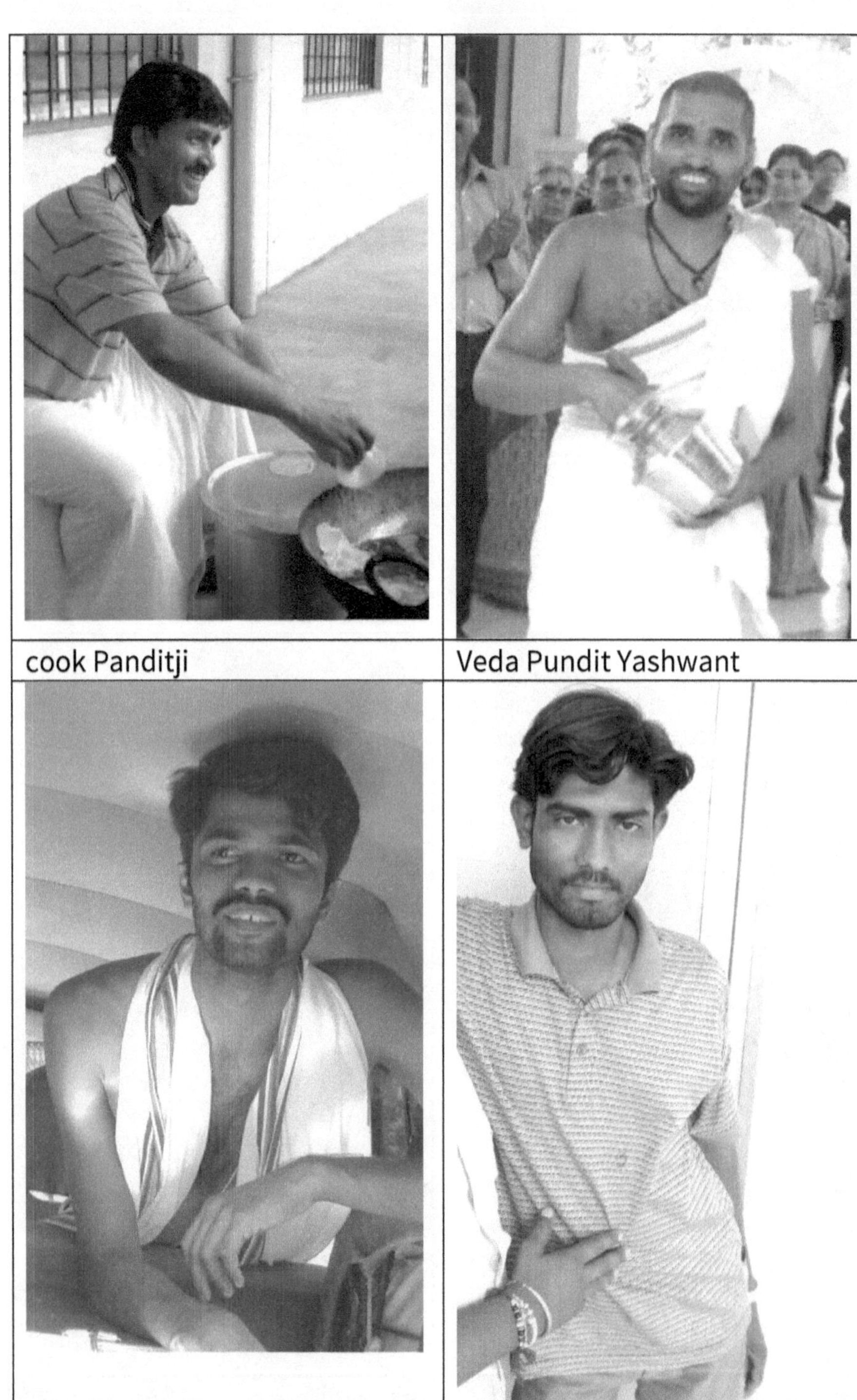

| cook Panditji | Veda Pundit Yashwant |
| Temple Priest Subhash | plumbing, maintenance guy |

Govindrajan	Lakshminarayan
Lady	Krishna

Group Photo outside Academic Block: 27 Dec 2014
Standing L to R: Priyadarshini, Yoga Instructor's wife
Sitting on chair L to R: Yashoda, **Mataji**
Sitting L to R: Seeta, Aruna
Front L to R: Children

Standing L to R: Ramila, Hemswaroop
Sitting on chair L to R: Yoga Instructor, Dinesh
Sitting L to R: Laxminarayan, Govindrajan, Ajay (hidden)
Front L to R: Ashwini, Panditji's son, Sucheendra

Celebrating Festivals

All festivals were celebrated with chanting, singing, decorations, and great food. All pupils and gurukul staff participated with gusto, and many times families from the city also joined.

Ganapati Sthapan and Visarjan

9:27am 9Sep2013. Ganapati Bappa Moraya, during parikrama.

9:30am 9Sep2013. Temple.

9:40am 9Sep2013. Chanting Ganesh Atharvashirsha.

10am 9Sep2013. Chanting Ganesh Atharvashirsha.

9:30am 18Sep2013. Walking to the Lake for Visarjan.

9:35am 18Sep2013. Singing Ganesh Aarti.

9:45am 18Sep2013. Final Visarjan in the deep waters of the lake.

4pm 18Sep2013 Bharat Nagar, Nagpur. Mataji, Mrs. Jichkar.

5pm 18Sep2013 Singing and Dancing, Nagpur. Ashwini.

18Sep2013 Govindrajan, Yajnavalkya Jichkar, during Ganapati Visarjan procession in Nagpur.

Noon 8Oct2015 Annadanam at Nagpur. Offering lunch to village folk.

Guru Poornima

9:30am 22Jul2013.

सदाशिवसमारम्भां
शङ्कराचार्यमध्यमाम् ।
अस्मदाचार्यपर्यन्तां
वन्दे गुरुपरम्पराम् ॥

9:50am 22Jul2013. Cook, Govindji, Rajuindran, Yashoda, Miki.

10am 17Jul2014. Offering Gurudakshina.

Walk to our Hanuman Temple every Poornima

Hanuman Temple was inaugurated at 9am on 23rd Apr 2013.

Noon 16Jan2014. Full Moon day.

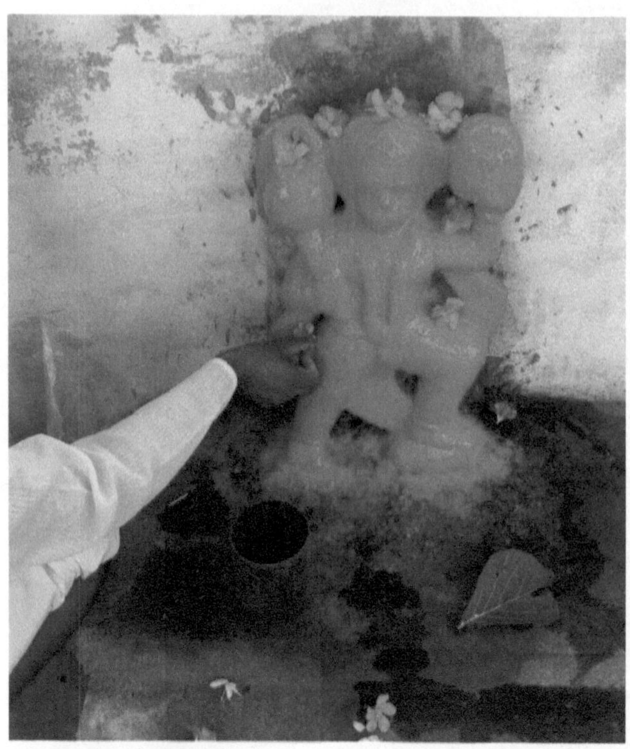

Noon 27Oct2015.

8am 4Apr2015. Full Moon day. Hanuman Jayanti, flag change.

5:30pm 26Feb2014. Full Moon day.

Diwali New Year Rangoli

6:30pm 4Nov2013. Outside Temple. Made by Seeta and Aruna.

Kartik Poornima Guru Nanak Birthday

8pm 17Nov2013. Kartik Poornima Guru Nanak birthday.

9pm 18Sep2013. Day of Ganesh Visarjan.

8pm 18Dec2013. Ardra Nakshatra, Rudra Puja.

Baisakhi Honoring FoodGrains

9:45am 14Apr2016. Worshipping Food and Foodgrains

6:30pm 14Apr2015. Classroom. Mataji and Rajuindran. Me and Venkat had gone to Kalmeshwar to get the assorted food items.

Weather Notes

Weather at the Gurukul was relatively comfortable for most part of the year, except for the summer months of April, May and June, when the Deccan plateau rocks began to boil and it was not advisable to stay. So all of us used to exit the Gurukul to continue our classes elsewhere. Before the beginning of the harsh season, a room cooler fitting task was carried out in each room.

The monsoon season of July and August was a welcome relief. It used to pour continuously for 3-4 days at a stretch, with dark clouds and no sunshine, but the showers were rather light. All of us had the big black umbrellas. I wore a raincoat for my cycling trips.

One important point to note here is that being situated in a deep forest, far from any light glare, the night sky is exceptionally clear, with the Milky Way galaxy clearly visible. Most constellations and stars are easily seen, and my telescope was a great help in spotting three moons of Jupiter and giving exceptional views of the Moon.

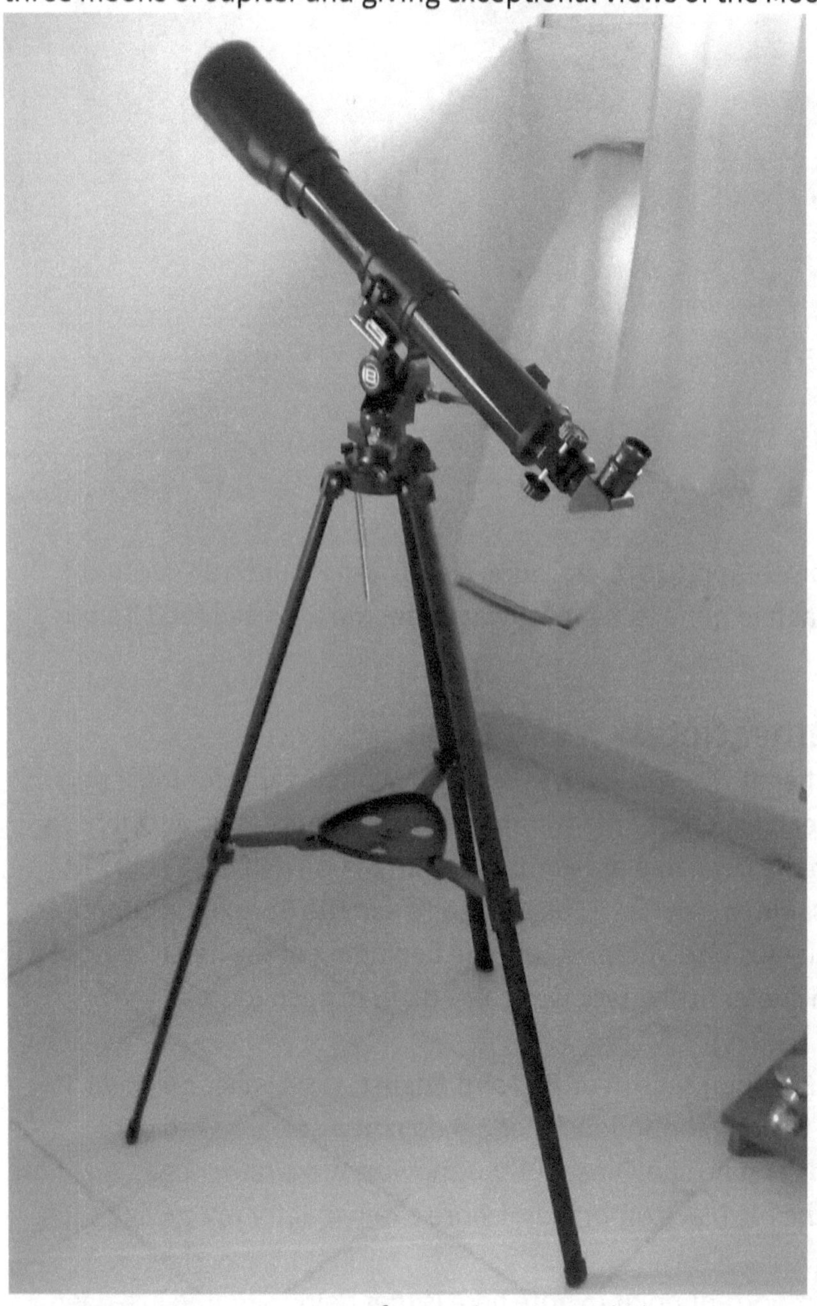

27Aug2014. Bresser 70mm refractor in my gurukul room.

Class Notes

Sample class notes of all discrete topics are given.

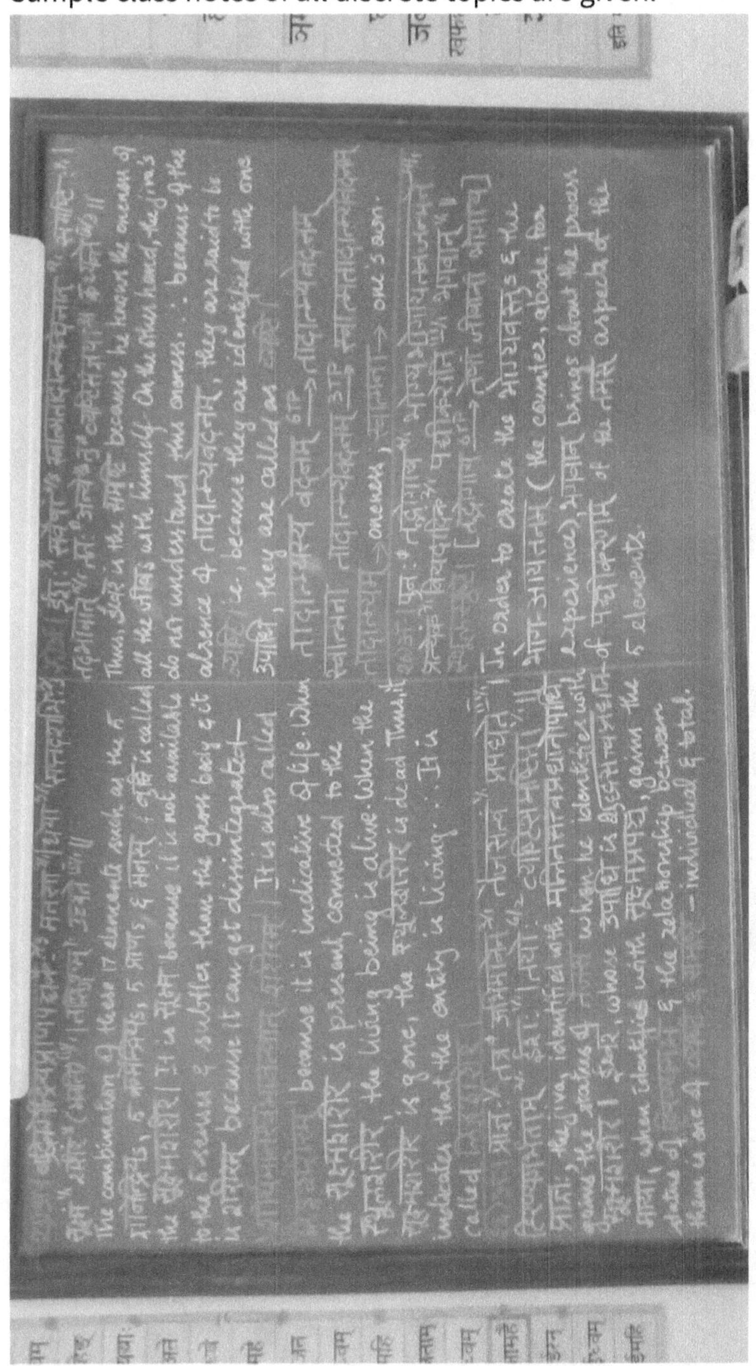

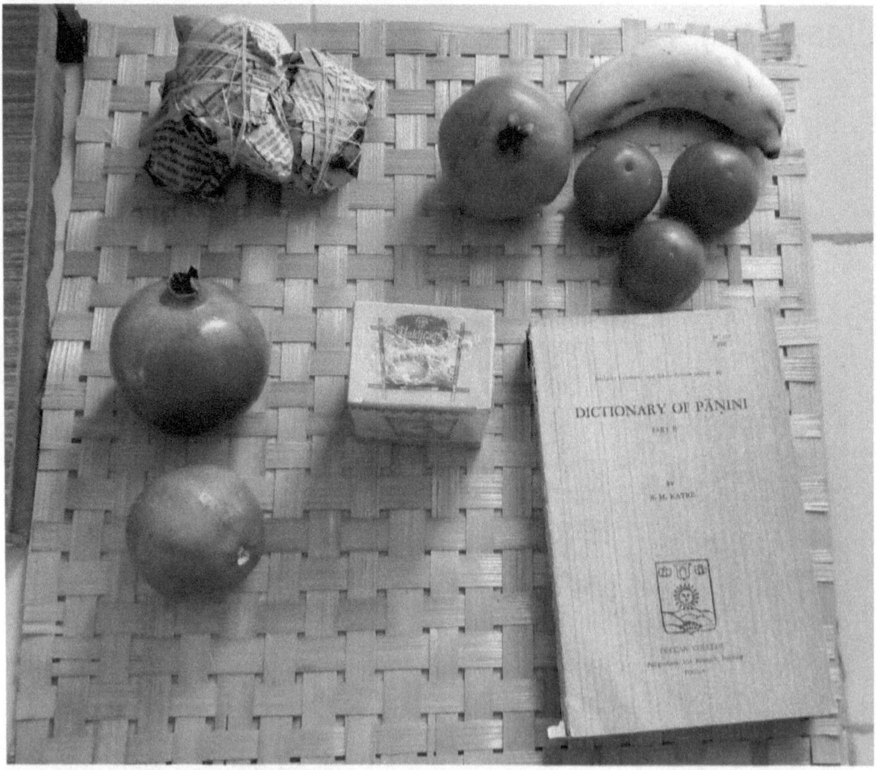
DICTIONARY OF PĀṆINI

THE AṢṬĀDHYĀYĪ OF PĀṆI
THE AṢṬĀDHYĀYĪ OF
THE AṢṬĀDHYĀYĪ OF
THE AṢṬĀDHYĀYĪ O
THE AṢṬĀDHYĀYĪ OF
Amul
Taaza
THE ART OF LIVING

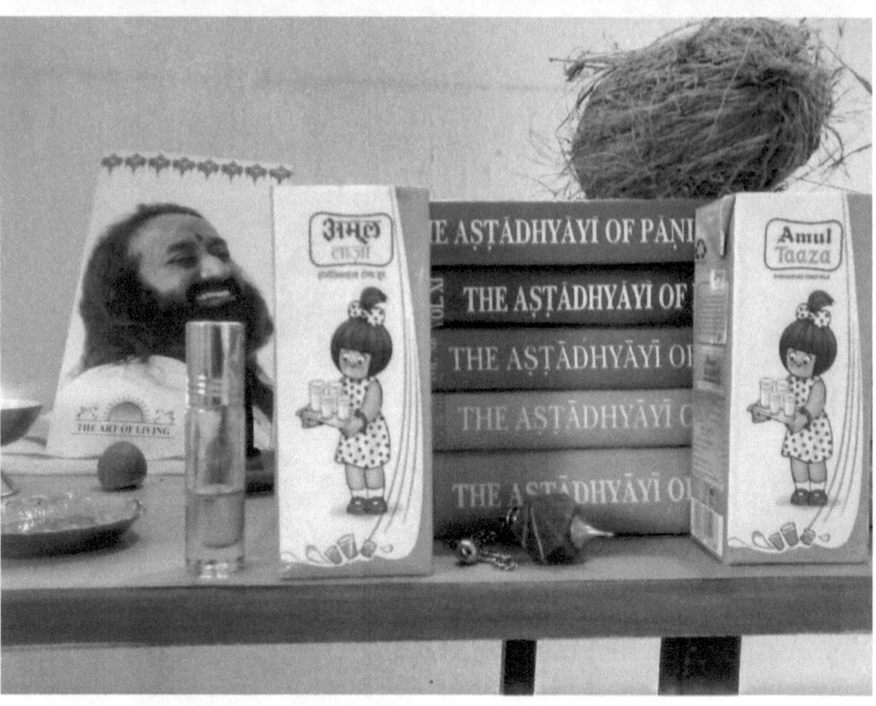

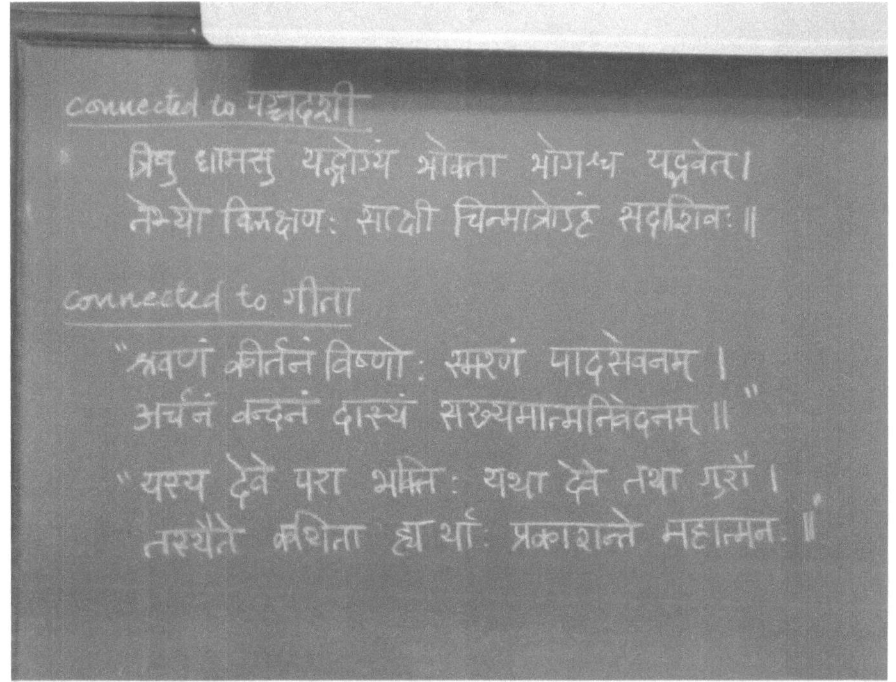

8Dec2014 Class Blackboard.

3pm 30Mar2015. Aruna, Seeta, Hemswaroop in classroom.

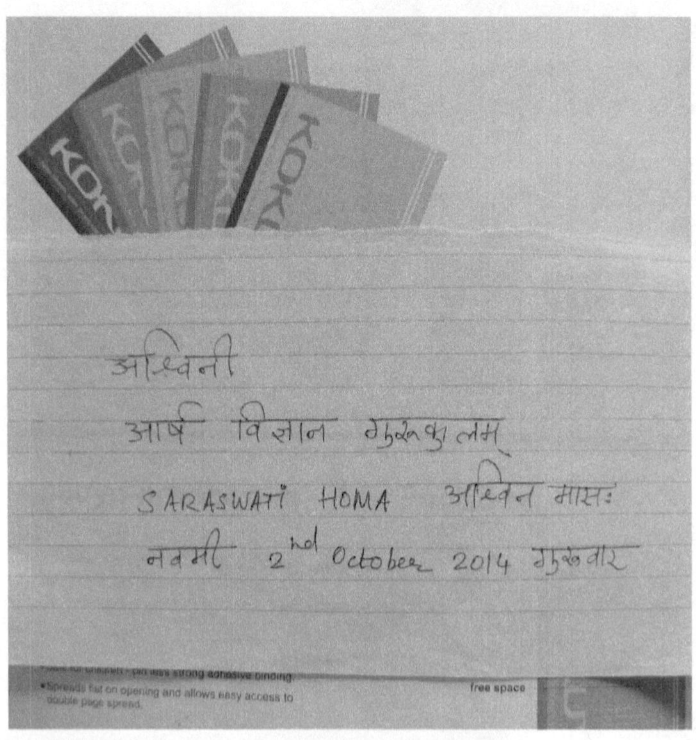
अश्विनी
आर्ष विज्ञान गुरुकुलम्
SARASWATI HOMA अश्विन मासः
नवमी 2nd October 2014 गुरुवार

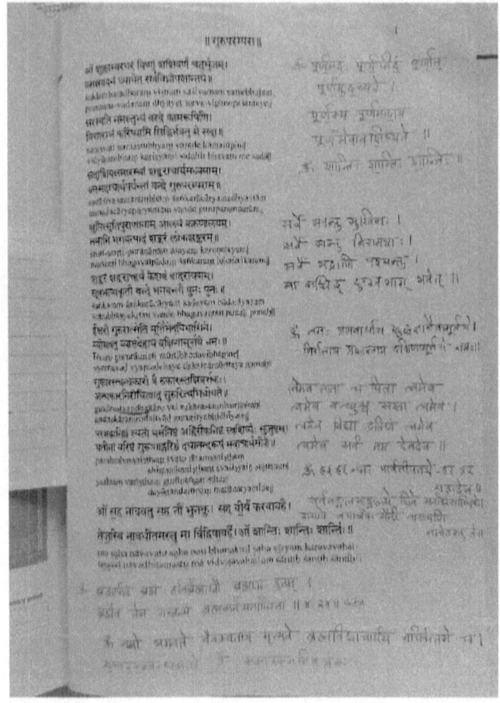

Title		Page.No.	Sign./Remarks
Tattvabodha	6:30 – 7:30 am		
Meditation	7:30 – 7:50 am		
Temple	8:00 – 8:30 am		
BF	8:30 – 8:45 am		
Sanskrit	9:15 – 10:15 am		
kathopanishad	11:15 – 12:15 noon		
Lunch	12:30 – 1pm		
स्वाध्याय:	till 3:30 pm		
TV session	3:30 pm – 4:15 pm		
Bhagvad Gita	4:30 – 5:30 pm		
Walk	5:30 – 6:30 pm		
Aarti/Temple/Bhajan	6:30 – 7:30 pm		
Dinner	8:00 – 8:30 pm		
Satsang class	8:30 – 9:15 pm		

जय गुरुदेव   9:15 am

SANSKRIT Text book page 18. Lesson 5. Instrumental & Dative (recipient)

A noun has 6 cases – kāraka –   Doer   object   instrument   recipient   point of origin   place
                                  1   2   3   4   5   6

The uses of the 4th case conjugation चतुर्थी विभक्ति: | Dative = Recipient = 4th case

1 → It is used to indicate the recipient of an act of giving

↳ सम्प्रदानम्

The book [Sabda Manjari] gives all the Noun forms whereas the book Dhaturupa Manjari gives all the Verb conjugations.

2 When one is angry the recipient of the anger is also called सम्प्रदानम् and is put in the 4th place.

जनक: पुत्राय कुप्यति | synonym कुध्यति

Not only anger, the recipient of any negative emotion is called सम्प्रदानम्

book white swan
Nick Hat Hands

दुर्जन: मित्राय द्रुह्यति | (to act against the friendship)
द्रोह → in the betrays eg. disciples when betray communist times, when neighbours informed police against you, it is the द्रोह

3. It is used to express the purpose of action
It is translated as "for the sake of"   तादर्थ्ये चतुर्थी
eg. planting a mango tree for the sake of next generation

जन: पुत्राय पौत्राय च वृक्षं आरोपयति

अर्जुन: धर्माय युद्धं कृतवान्   arjuna fought for the sake of dharma

माता पुत्रेभ्य: पाकं करोति | जन: पुत्रेभ्य: कूप

* Derivation of भावकर्मप्रयोग: ।

    We will see the derivational process of the भावकर्म-प्रयोग: as against the derivational process of कर्तरि-प्रयोग:

    The derivational process for the कर्मणि and भावे are same. therefore, we refer as a भावकर्मप्रयोग:।

कर्तरि प्रयोग:	भावकर्मप्रयोग:।
1. The roots have the conjugational differences. That is the division of the ten गण's are valid only in the कर्तरि प्रयोग:।	1. The division of the form of the 10 गण's are not therefore, भावकर्मप्रयोग:।
2. The division of roots into परस्मैपदी, आत्मनेपदी, and उभयपदी are valid.	2. Here only आत्मनेपद विङ्-प्रत्यय are used.
3. We have to consider गुण and वृद्धि substitutions.	3. No need to consider (नियमेन) गुण and वृद्धि substitution generally. Note: In भावे प्रयोग we have only one form, that is m/i. singular

भावकर्म-प्रयोगः ।

→ कर्मणि-प्रयोगः च भावे प्रयोगः ।

11/3/14. Tuesday.
9:15 am

भावकर्म - तिङन्त प्रयोगः ।

Passive and passive Impersonal usage of a verb.

These are three kinds of तिङन्तप्रयोग - usage of the verb.
1. कर्तरि-प्रयोगः - The verb denotes the कर्ता (Agent).
2. कर्मणि-प्रयोगः - The verb denotes the कर्म (object).
3. भावे-प्रयोगः - The verb denotes the भावार्थः = the abstract
meaning of the root.

Example:
देवदत्तः अपूपं खादति । कर्तरिप्रयोगः: Devadatta eats am apupa.
देवदत्तेन अपूपः खाद्यते । कर्मणि प्रयोगः: An Apupa is eaten by Devdatta.
देवदत्तेन आस्यते । भावे प्रयोगः: Devadatta sits (The sentence
is in भावे प्रयोगः।) sitting by Devadatta.

All the roots will have कर्तरि प्रयोगः ।
Only सकर्मक roots will have कर्मणि प्रयोगः ।
अकर्मक roots will have भावे प्रयोगः ।
When the object is not mentioned then
सकर्मक roots can also have भावे प्रयोगः ।

Ex: देवदत्तेन खाद्यते ।

In English in the modern times there is no
use of the Passive Impersonal (भावे) but in संस्कृतम्
भावेप्रयोग is very commonly used. Because of the
background of the vedanta. In general in Sanskrit
the कर्मणि and भावे प्रयोगs are used very extensively (प्रायेण)
because we have to give up our कर्तृत्वम् the कर्मणि and
भावे are used in preference (प्राधान्य). Instead of saying
अहं गतवान् or अहं खादितवान् it is more natural to say
मया गतम् व् मया खादितम् ।

* Actual process of Derivation of भावकर्मप्रयोगः ।

The root is taken down for derivation, the आत्मनेपद्-प्रत्यय corresponding (तदअनुसार) to the object in person & number is added to the root. Instead of the गणविकरणम् - शप्, now the प्रत्यय 'यक्' comes immediately after the root.

The प्रत्यय - 'यक्' being a कित्-प्रत्यय can not cause गुण or वृद्धि to the root. Then all the elements are added we get the form

खाद् + ते यक् → खाद् + यक् + ते → खाद्यते ।

| कर्तरि | बालाः | ओदनम् | खादन्ति । |
| कर्मणि | ओदनः | बालैः | खाद्यते । |

| कर्तरि | त्वम् | ओदनम् | खादसि । |
| कर्मणि | ओदनः | त्वया | खाद्यते । |

| कर्तरि | अहम् | ओदनं | खादामि । |
| कर्मणि | ओदनः | मया | खाद्यते । |

Once we derive खाद्यते. [खाद्य] is the अर्क for the all other forms. and add the other affixes and derive the form.

9:45am
19/03/19

* विभक्ति in भावकर्म-प्रयोगः

1. कर्मणि प्रयोगः since the verb denotes the कर्म (obj), कर्म is denoted therefore, कर्म will be in 1st case. कर्ता will be undenoted and will therefore, take 3rd case. करणम्, सम्प्रदानम्, अपादानम् and अधिकरणम् are all undenoted in भावकर्मप्रयोग as in कर्तरिप्रयोगः therefore, will be in the same विभक्ति as in कर्तरिप्रयोगः that is 3rd, 4th, 5th & 7th respectively.

जौगृ निद्राक्षये । १८c. प. सेट् to awake. — जक्षादिगण

Note [ ]
Date — 1/4/15
Page —

गुण substitution ०

सूत्र०॥ मिदेर्गुणः ॥ ७.३.८२ ॥ शिति अङ्गस्य [इकः — इको गुणवृद्धि । १.१.३]

वृ०॥ मिदेः अङ्गस्य इकः गुणः भवति शिति प्रत्यये परतः ।

अ०॥ मिदेः अङ्गस्य इकः गुणः शिति ।

Transo॥ This सूत्र says, the इक् belonging to the root 'मिद्' takes गुण substitution, when a शित्-प्रत्यय follows. Now we have 4 roots as which have the form of मिद् ।

15/2	त्रिमिदाँ	स्नेहने	1c	आत्मनेपद्.	सेट्	मेदते ।
19/1	मिदृ	मेधाहिंसनयोः	1c	उभय.	सेट्	मेदति । मेदते ।
31/2	त्रिमिदाँ	स्नेहने	4c	परस्मैः	सेट्	मेद्यति ।
41/1	मिदि	स्नेहने	10 c	मिन्द्यति । मिन्दयते । मिन्दति (३)

(द्वितीयस्य ष्णा०: ७.१.५८)

The two first conjugation root would have taken गुण-substitution by पुगन्तलघूपधस्य । ७.३.८६ ॥ without a problem. But the 4th conjugation root 'मिद्' would not have taken गुण because श्यन् being अपित् सार्वधातुकम् would have become ङित् and no गुण would have taken place. But we have the form → मेद्यति' also. Therefore, Pāṇini made this सूत्र as specific to मिद् । Whether शप् or श्यन् follows. Therefore, now whether it is a 1st conjugation root or 4th conjugation root, the root 'मिद्' will take गुण only by this सूत्र !

<u>Note :</u> The 10th conjugation root 'मिद्' being इदित् root will get 'नुम्' augment by the सूत्र इदितो नुम् धातोः । ७.१.५८ Then will get स्वार्थे णिच् । णिच् not being शित् Therefore this सूत्र will not apply.

Visiting Faculty

10:30am 15Oct2013. Swami Chitsvarupananda in the Guest House. He was very engaging and filled us with confidence.

Dr. Karaikudi S. Subramanian, an exponent of the Veena, taught us raaga and music. https://www.brhaddhvani.com/

Swami Shivaprakashananda Saraswati taught us Sanskrit Grammar derivation of Nouns, and took classes on Ishavasya Upanishad. He was a master of chanting and correct pronunciation.

https://vibhufoundation.com/

Shruti Sapre visited us every Saturday and also on Festivals. She taught us Bhagavad Gita chanting, and took revision of Sanskrit Grammar from the Upanishad and Grammar texts.

Flora and Fauna

8:30am 5Jan2014. A thorny medicinal plant at 19Km Oranges Orchard turn. Below – A bark in winter 5pm 23Dec2013

4:40pm 25Dec2013 Blue Jay

5:56am 27Apr2014 Sunrise during walk to Dorli.

6am 27Apr2014 Dorli halt after walk.

Noon 29Jan2014. View from nearby Hilltop overlooking Lake.

8:30am 5Jan2014

9am 6Apr2014

7:40am 8Dec2013. Teak tree leaf.

8:45am 8Dec2013. Venkataramana Ashwini Ganesh shadows.

6pm 10Oct2013. Climbing the Hill just behind Gurukul. Swami Chitsvarupananda, Ajay, Ganesh.

8am 17Nov2013. Cherries.

5:30pm 17Dec2013. Gorakshan cows passing on the road to lake.

3pm 29Oct2015. Rainbow from Terrace of Boys Kutir.

9:35am 1Feb2015. Cabbage field near IMT after Dorli walking towards Mohali, on Katol Nagpur highway.

6:40am 16Feb2014. Sugarcane field

10am 23Mar2014. Chandrabhaga river lake during walk.

117

8am 2Mar2014. Breakfast halt at Kohli on the Katol Nagpur highway during walk. We spot a Chilli field.

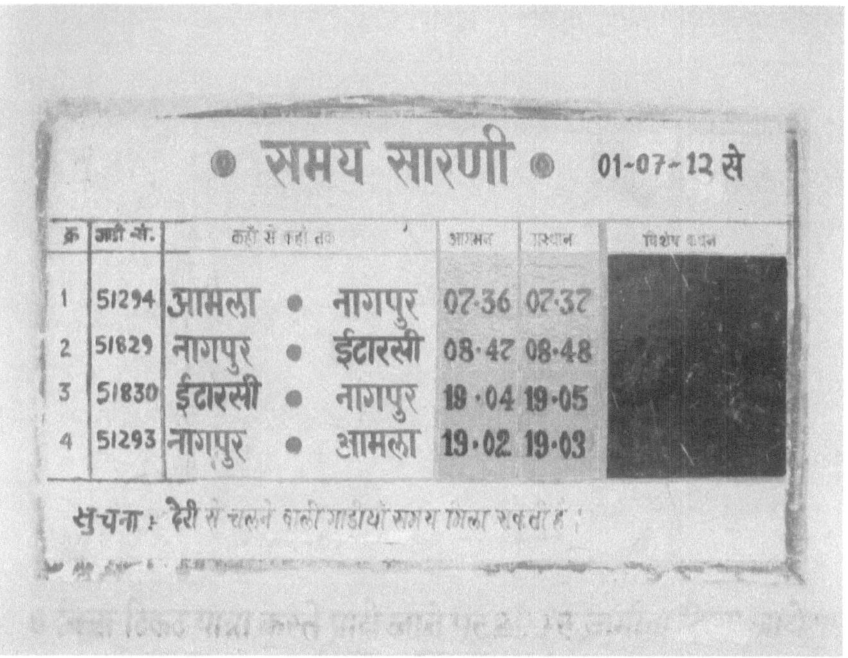

After our walk, we boarded the local train at Kohli a couple of times, either going to Nagpur, or going towards Katol.

Noon 16Jan2014. We spotted Neelgai.

Apart from this, other animals noticed at different times were deer, wild-boar, rabbit, leopard, in the jungles surrounding the Gurukul.

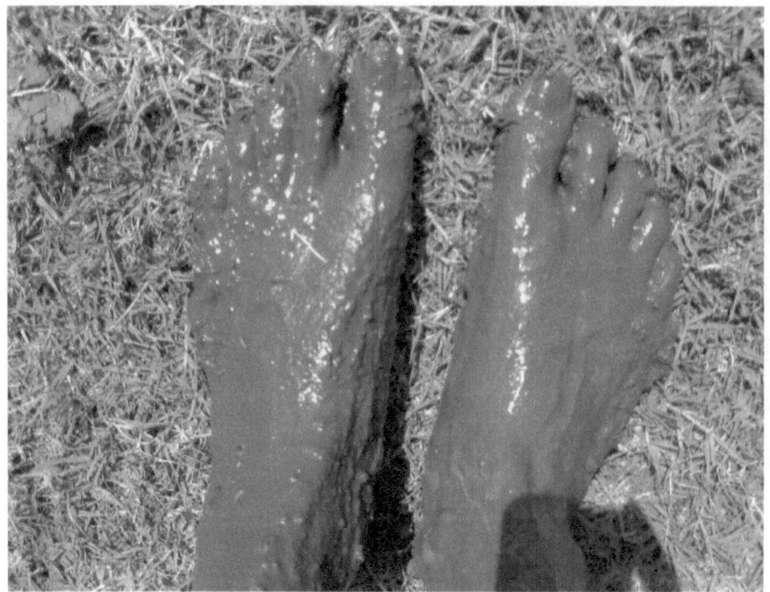

10:21am 23Mar2014. Feet in rich alluvial river-bed soil.

Yogasana Classes

A Yoga instructor from Iyengar Yoga Mumbai branch visited and took Yogasana classes over 4 days. All participated enthusiastically. For the first time I did the Sirsasana, and then there was a slip and a fall! All Ok.

11am 26Dec2014. Yoga Instructor, his wife (right), Ramila (center).

12pm 2Apr2015. SuryaNamaskar Asana Ashvasanchalana.

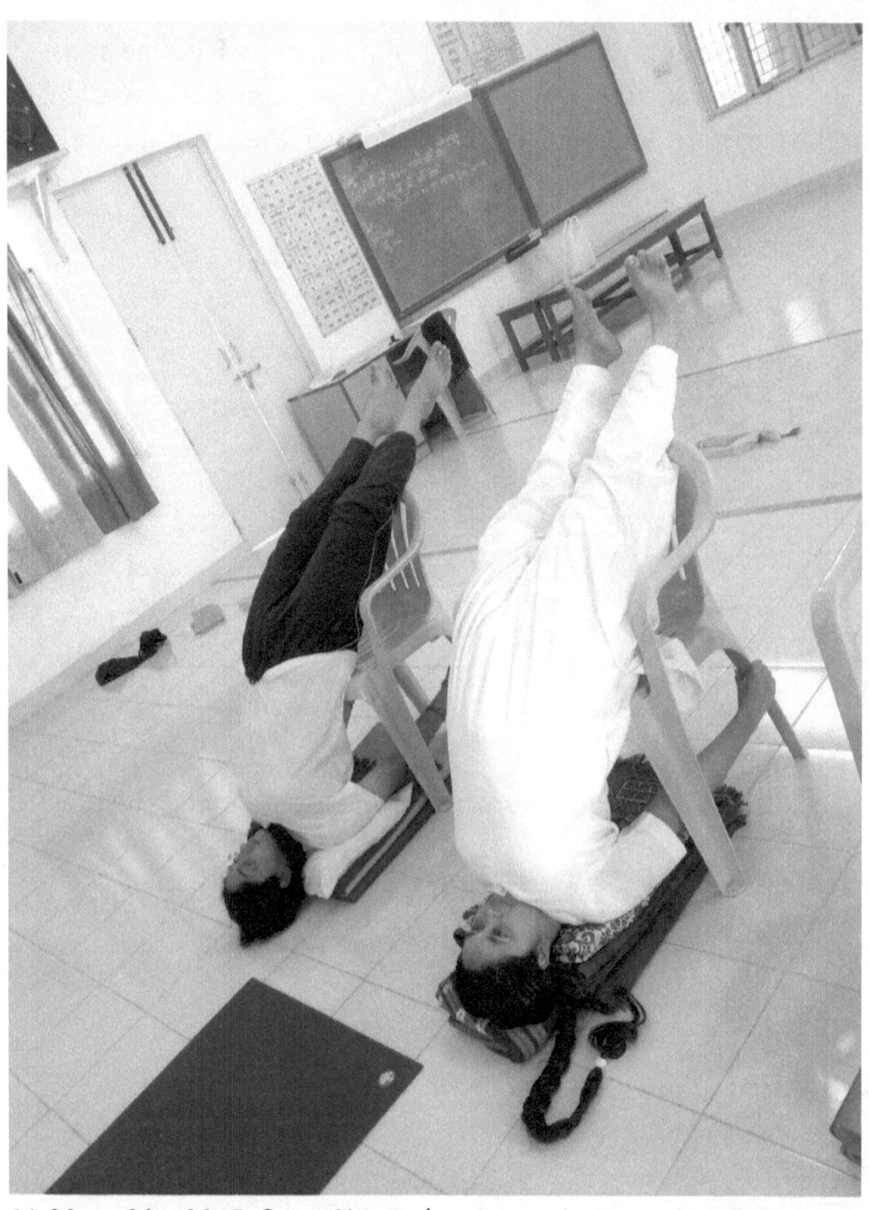

11:20am 3Apr2015. SuryaNamaskar Asana Sarvangasana.

Pujya Swami Centerspread

3:30pm 7Feb2014. An outing to a nearby village festival.

8:12am 14Nov2009. Mataji with Pujya Swamiji upon his visit to Nagpur Gurukulam during an earlier course.

Pujya Swamiji Dayananda Saraswati

Pujya Swamini Brahmaprakasananda Saraswati

9:30am 15Feb2015. Meeting Shree Shree Anantanand Guru Maa.

Planned Outings

Mataji's Saturday visits to Nagpur for Classes

Sometimes, some of us also took this opportunity to visit Nagpur for personal shopping and outing.

Narayan Bet Pune Summer Classes 2014

April, May, June of 2014 was spent at the Narayan Maharaj Dutt Ashram on the outskirts of Pune. All Gurukul pupils and Mataji boarded the train and reached Pune. There was an exciting event at the Pune station, while unloading the luggage I found my study books bag was missing, and Hemswaroop came to my aid as she loaned her set to me for the time being. Pune arrival 30April2014

It was a dry arid area, and the outskirts of the Ashram were full of thorny bush and low hedges. On walks we sighted deer, peacocks, and weaver bird nests. We also visited some Mango orchards and collected loads of juicy fruit.

नागपुर पुणे
12114
12113

Mataji, Ajay, Priya, Govindrajan, Ramila, NarayanAshramTrustee.

8:45am 10May2014 Narayan Ashram Temple. Kedgaon-Bet, 55Km from Pune.

Our accommodation was in a village like hut having six rooms. Me and Ajay shared the room at the entrance. It was here that we watched the live election results of the May elections and the swearing-in of the Indian PM.

The Satyanarayan Puja was the major rite performed here with many pundits worshipping and chanting together, and we pupils also took part in the same.

8:45am 14Jun2014 Classroom. Dinesh doing a grammar verb derivation on the blackboard.

Alandi Mauli Gyaneshwar Trip

During our summer vacation in June, our entire class alongwith Mataji went on many sightseeing trips, including Shirdi and Shani Shingnapur.

4pm 10Jun2014. Alandi Temple town of Saint Gyaneshwar.

6:45pm 10Jun2014. Gyaneshwar Temple and Lake, Alandi.

Prati Balaji Temple Ketkawale Pune

An exact replica of the world famous Tirupati Balaji Temple, surrounded by folds-of-hills on the outskirts of Pune.

We were pleasantly surprised at the availability of juicy fruit in the temple vicinity.

10:45am 2Jun2014. Mango Fig Guava fresh fruits.

Manjakudi Ashram Summer Classes 2015

April and May of 2015 were spent at the birthplace of Swami Dayananda Saraswati, the AVG center in Manjakudi, Tamil Nadu.

4:16pm 24May2015. Manjakuddi Study Centre.

10:10am 26May2015. Mataji Ashwini Laxminarayan Aruna Seeta.

12:56pm 26May2015. Lunch time at Dining Hall, Manjakuddi.

Kumbakonam Temple Visit

Our entire class with Mataji visited many temples in Kumbakonam in June 2015. Also attended a Homa Ritual at a temple.

Brihad-Isvara Temple Visit

9:50pm 10Jun2015. Brihadishvara Nandi Thanjavur.

9am 10Jun2015. Hemswaroop, Ashwini at Brihadishvara Thanjavur.

Buying Vegetables from Nagpur Mandi

Mataji chose me and Ajay to accompany her to the Nagpur subzimandi for vegetable and grocery procurement for kitchen. We used to drive there once a month on Saturdays, spend a couple of hours in shopping, and drive back with the heavily loaded fresh vegetables. The girls then used to separate and arrange them, and help the cook to stock them in the cold-storage.

I maintained an excel spreadsheet for accounting.

Arsha Vijnana Gurukulam Grocery		Date	12/08/2014	
Gurukul/Temple/Pathshala		for month of Aug 2014		
		Packing 1	Packing 2	Packing 3
SN	Item	Qty Kg	Qty Kg	Qty Kg
1	Chana (dalia)	3	-	-
2	Chana dal	50	-	-
3	Chana sabuth desi	6	4	1
5	chawlai - Barbati	6	3	1
7	cooking salt - cow brand 1kg pack	30	2	3
8	coconut	-	60 nos	-
9	dhania seeds	3	-	-
10	green peas	3	3	1
11	ground nuts - small red	5	4	1
12	gud - jaggery - chemical free	2	10	2
13	haldi powder (0.5kg pack)	3	-	250 gm
14	hing solid	50 gms	-	-
15	jeera - 1kg pack	4	0.5	200 gm
16	lijjat papad	6 pkt	-	-
17	matki	6	-	1
18	methi seeds	1	-	-
19	moong sabuth	6	3	1
20	moong dal with skin	6	-	1
24	poha - thick	25	-	5
25	rahi - mustard seeds - clean	3	0.5	200 gm
26	rajma	4	-	-
27	rava - thick	15	-	2
28	Red chillies - whole	2	0.25	-
29	Rice plain	100	100	-
30	Sabudana	6	-	1

Personal Time
GuruPuja Havan Kriya

I enjoyed doing Guru Puja.
Also did Agnihotra regularly in my Kutir.

Me and Ajay used to do Long Sudarshan Kriya follow-ups regularly.

Vacuuming Printing Publishing

I had a small vacuum cleaner and used to clean my room thoroughly every fortnight.

I also had a Deskjet color printer, and took Sanskrit Grammar handouts regularly for use in class.

Teaming up with Venkataramana, our "Dhatupatha of Panini" book was typed on my Acer Notebook. It got published during our stay in Gurukul.

My "Bhagavad Gita for Chanting" book was also conceptualized here, taking cues from Shruti's Saturday chanting classes. Yashoda helped in writing verses with pause at 8 quarters, which me and Hemswaroop later typed on our laptop.

Memorable visit of dear Family and Friends

I got a wonderful surprise one autumn evening, when at 11pm in the night, my dear friend Jagjit Singh and cousin Dr Manoj visited us from Ludhiana. They spent the night rather comfortably in my sparsely furnished room, visited the Temple, had lunch in the Kitchen, attended Mataji's early morning Bhagavad Gita lecture, and Shruti's Saturday Grammar revision class.

They brought us wonderful presents, including a saffron shawl for Mataji and a cream shawl for Hemswaroop, and gave us the strong feeling that our family back home had richly blessed us.

Hemswaroop's Mumbai Mumma also visited another time, and we spent a happy hour at the lake, chatting away. Priyadarshini's young son's visit gave us all a cheery time too. My Mangrulpir family Abhay, and Mohan, Babita, Manoj and Komal, also visited a couple of times and kept any feeling of loneliness at bay.

Bicycle rides to Nagpur

I bought a bicycle, the black Hero Jet, and bicycled regularly. During evenings, I rode up to Dorli, or just beyond to the vegetable market at Kohli.

On Sundays I used to cycle all the way to Nagpur, a distance of 45Km, and felt happy buying a carton of Amul Milk, containing 24 bottles. On one of these trips, me and Venkat made friends with a retired government official Kewal, who introduced us to the South Korean spine massage bed.

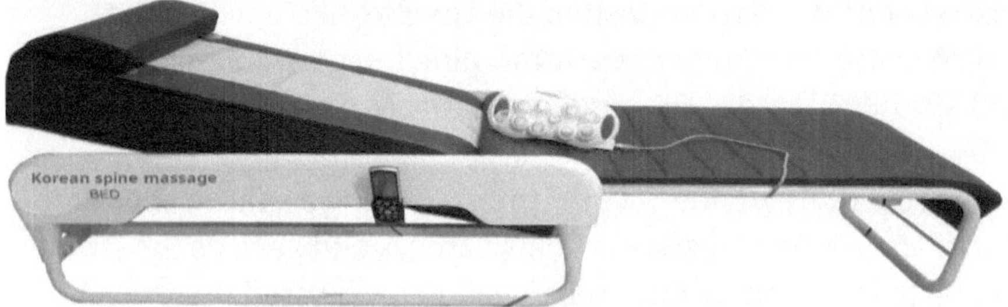

4pm 15Aug2015 Kewal taking us around in Nagpur.

Bus rides to Katol

On weekends, some of the group enjoyed visiting Katol for doing grocery and stationery shopping.

Usually me, Venkat, Ganesh, and Sucheendra used to catch the bone joint straining rickety bus from the Dorli Bazargaon road at 2Km from Gurukul. It took us to the market place of Katol a distance of 25Km, where we roamed the brass-market for utensils, grocery market for dry fruits, and stationery shops for notebooks and paper. Then we had to catch the return bus in time. There was only one bus service every day that came till the Gurukul, other buses passed by Dorli towards Nagpur, but these were few and far between. Dorli was 9Km away from Gurukul, and so we used to hire Sanjay for his auto service.

Nagpur Halts upon Arrival by Train

On my trips abroad, when I returned to Nagpur by train, I used to visit Wasudha's home for breakfast, before proceeding to the Gurukul. I had made her acquaintance during a Long Kriya follow-up at the Vidarbha Ashram.

Basic Course

I had the good fortune of introducing the Basic Course to Hemswaroop. Later during a visit to Art of Living Ashram Bangalore, Venkataramana did the residential course there. So did Yashoda. Ganesh visited me one afternoon during Guruji's satsang at Ashram. Priyadarshini also expressed her interest in doing the course.

Swami Chitsvarupananda had visited the Ashram Gurukul in Bangalore, and Swami Shivaprakashananda had shared the dais with Guruji on one occasion.

Guruji's Visit Sand Dunes Melghat 15/1/2014

One evening, me, Ajay and Venkat went for Guruji's darshan at the house of an Art of Living Trustee in Nagpur. Sri Sri was so loving, and filled us with bliss and enthusiasm.

Art of Living Ashram Nagpur 19/1/2014

The Vidarbha Art of Living Ashram is located in Dahegaon, near Kalmeshwar, 18Km from Nagpur. It is around 25 Km from Gurukul. We visited for the Upanayanam course.

8am 23Feb2014. Celebrating Foundation Day of Vidarbha Ashram.

Nasik Kumbh Mela Visit Sep 2015

Kumbh Mela, Godavari kund Shahi Snan day 25Sep2015.

Guruji's Visit BodhGaya Ashram 12/3/2014

I visited the Art of Living Ashram in Bodh Gaya for Holi with Guruji.

Home coming for Golden Jubilee 22/3/2014

I had a most memorable event in my life, when my Mummy and Papa celebrated their 50th marriage anniversary golden jubilee. It was a gala affair, with almost all my dear friends and relatives and cousins joining.

My Mummy and Papa looked cheerful and fit, and danced gaily dressed in handsome robes.

8am 22Mar2014. Papa, Preeti, Mummy, at the golden jubilee anniversary celebrations, TnG Hotel, Patiala.

Maheshwar Somayagya Visit Feb 2015

10am 8Feb2015. Agnihotra, TryambakamHoma Maheshwar, Indore. Yahswantji from Gurukul was there in Vedic chanting pandits team. The sixth Somayag named Atiratra was held at the Homa Therapy Goshala from 3rd to 8th Feb 2015. https://fivefoldpathmission.org/

Alipurduar Wildlife Sanctuary Visit July 2015

8am 23Jul2015. Wildlife Sanctuary, Alipurduar with Dr. Somnath.

Gujarat Temple Visit Aug 2015

I visited many temples, including Dwarka and Somnath with my
friends from the Art of Living Gujarat Ashram.

9:56am 5Aug2015. Bhalka Tirth, Dehotsarg Golok Dham, final
resting place of Lord Krishna.

Pushpa Maa modern day Panini Oct 2015

16Oct2015. Pushpa Maa's autograph. Panini Shodh Sansthan, Bilaspur Chattisgarh.

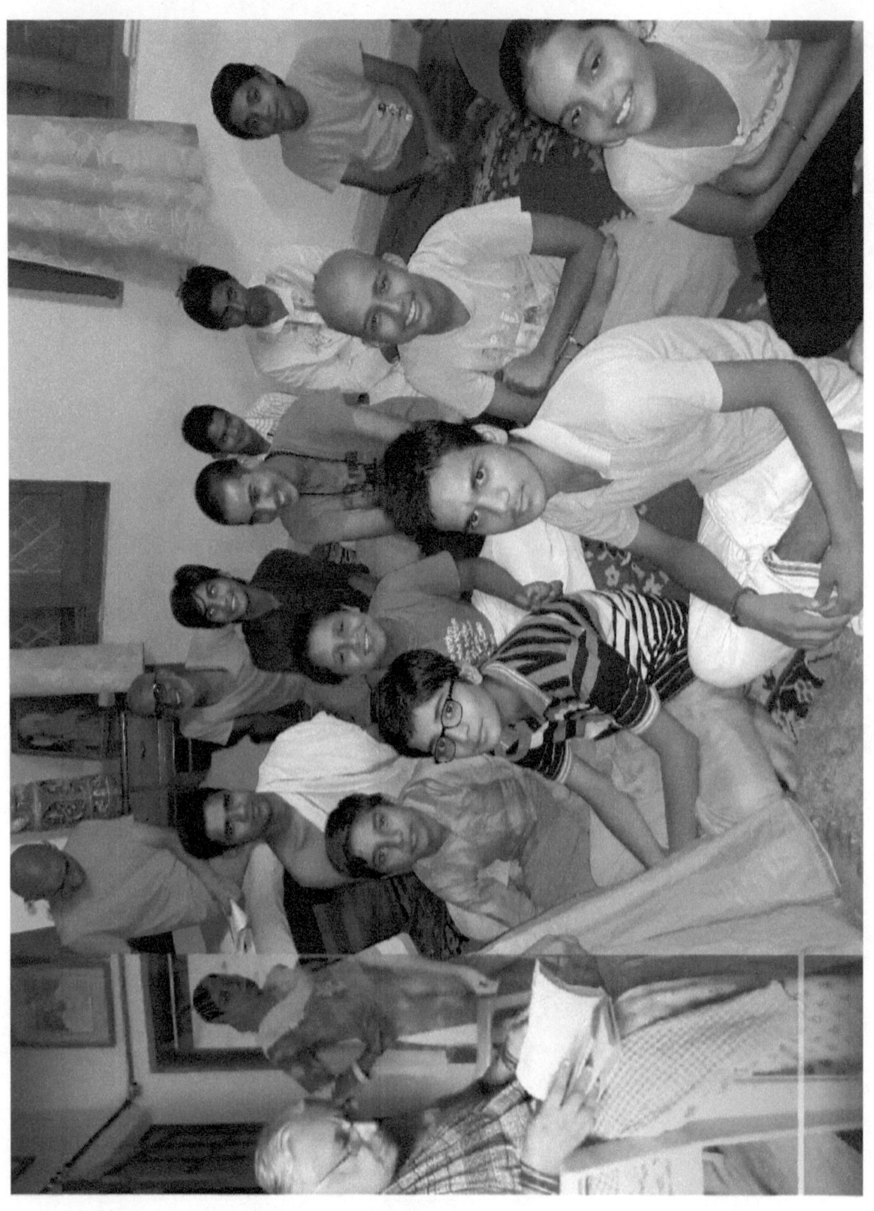

Puspha Maa's Ashtadhyayi class underway.

https://pushpadikshit.wordpress.com/

Anantanand GuruMaa's Nagpur Visit 22/12/2015

Hemswaroop Satyaswaroop, GuruMaa, Mathadeesh, MuniMaharaj
Front row – Divyaswaroop, Ashwini.

Shree Shree Maa Anantanand Ashram, Pardeshvar Mahadev Temple, Vahelal, Ahmedabad is a renowned Ayurvedic center.

AOL Teachers' Special AMC Dec 2015

There was a Punjab Art of Living Teachers' Special Advanced Meditation Course at Doraha, Punjab. It was conducted by Swami Paramtej and assisted by Gauri-Sharada.

It was a forerunner to the upcoming World Culture Festival extravaganza, the 35th anniversary of The Art of Living foundation.

World Cultural Festival Mar 2016

Swami Harihara came from the Art of Living Ashram to personally invite Mataji as a dignitary for the prestigious World Cultural Festival at New Delhi, 11-13 March 2016.

I had the opportunity to participate on stage in the Ashram Yoga performance on 13th March, in front of a million spectators! Guruji was especially pleased with the Yoga troupe, and waved encouragingly at us all.

My entire family joined in the audience, including my parents, sisters, nephew and niece. On day one just before the start of the musical extravaganza, there was a dazzling rainbow that delighted the hearts of all.

Sewing and Stitching

We used to get a set of clothes annually, and sometimes we visited a local village home to get some stitching work done.

Noon, 6Dec2014 Doing some stitching work.

Srauta Rites Treta Agni at Jichkar Home

The three havan kund for Yagya at Jichkarji's home. At West is Circular = Garhpatyagni, at South is Semicircular = Dakshinagni, at East is Square = Ahavaniya.

Meeting Pujya Swamiji at Rishikesh Sep 2015
Swamiji chatted with all of us individually and richly blessed us.

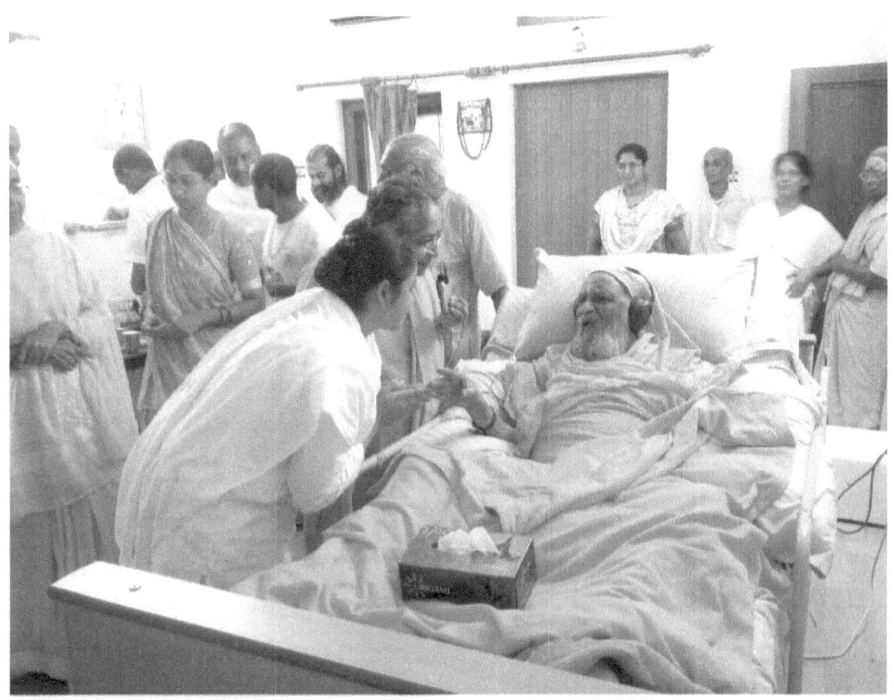

12:55am 12Sep2015. Pujya Swamiji's darshan by all the Pupils.

6am 11Sep2015. Meditating on the Ganges river bank.

11am 9Sep2015. Lecture Hall Rishikesh Ashram. Standing: Aruna Seeta. Sitting back row: Priya Shruti Ramila Laxminarayan Yashoda Govindrajan Dinesh. Front: Hemswaroop Ganesh Rajuindran.

We all had darshan of PM during this trip.

Graduation Valedictory Function 13-15 Apr 2016

11:23am 13Apr2016 Aruna, Mataji, Seeta. Guru Puja, Academic Hall.

12:06pm 15Apr2016 Ashwini, Mataji. Academic Hall.

11:41am 15Apr2016 Priyadarshini receiving graduation certificate.

11:39am 15Apr2016 Ashwini receiving graduation certificate.

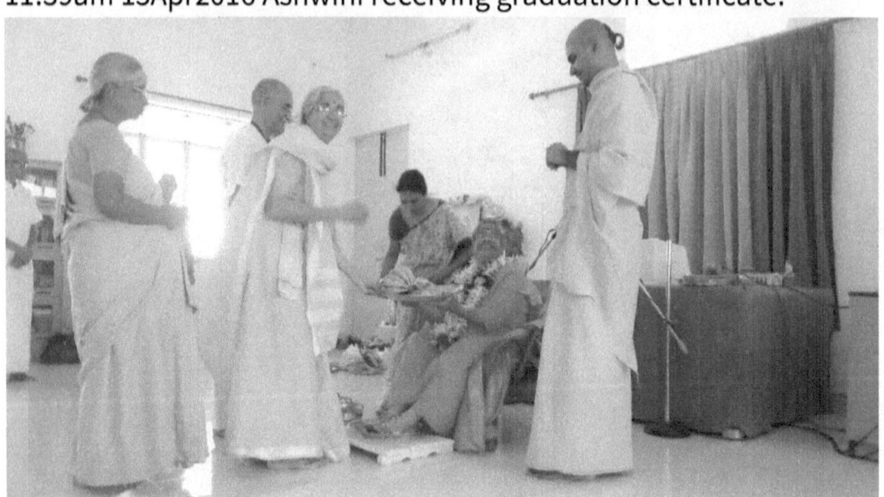

11:16am 13Apr2016 Guru Puja.

Graduating Class: 15 April 2016
Standing L to R: Ramila, Dinesh, Ajay, Ganesh
Sitting L to R: Yashoda, **Mataji**
Front L to R: Priyadarshini, Laxminarayan, Hemswaroop,

Graduating Class: 15 April 2016
Rajuindran, Ashwini, Lady

Seeta, Aruna

Standing: Govindji, Dash, Ajay, Laxminarayan, Ganesh, Govindrajan, Dinesh, Ashwini, Sw., Vinay

Sitting: Kavikulaguru Univ Swamiji, Swamini, **Mataji**, Mrs Jichkar, Yashoda

Front: Shruti, Seeta, Lady, Aruna, Ramila, Hemswaroop, Priyadarshini with son

Vedanta and Sanskrit Course Certificate

Dr. Shrikant Jichkar Memorial

ARSHA VIJNANA GURUKULAM

Vedapuri, Nagpur

This is to certify that **Ashwini Kumar Aggarwal** has received instruction in VEDANTA as detailed below during the THREE YEAR RESIDENTIAL COURSE IN VEDANTA AND SANSKRIT, which commenced on January 15, 2013.

[Approximately 1500 Hours of Instruction]

Upaniṣads

Kathopaniṣad — with Śaṅkarabhāṣyam and the gloss of Ānandagiri

Kenopaniṣad — with Śaṅkarabhāṣyam and the gloss of Ānandagiri [Padabhāṣya]

Mundakopaniṣad — with Śaṅkarabhāṣyam and the gloss of Ānandagiri

Taittiriyopaniṣad — with Śaṅkarabhāṣyam and the gloss, Vanamālā and Vidyāranyadīpikā

Chāndogyopaniṣad Chapter VI and VII and some other selected sections

— with Śaṅkarabhāṣyam and the gloss of Ānandagiri

Brhadāranyakopaniṣad Chapter I Section 4 & some other selected sections

— with Śaṅkarabhāṣyam and the gloss of Ānandagiri

Māndūkyopaniṣad & Kārikā — with Śaṅkarabhāṣyam and the gloss of Ānandagiri

Īśāvāsyopaniṣad — with Śaṅkarabhāṣyam and the gloss of Ānandagiri

Kaivalyopaniṣad — with the gloss of Maniprabhā

Bhagavadgītā

With Śaṅkarabhāṣyam and the gloss of Ānandagiri and the gloss of Bhāṣyotkarṣadīpikā

Brahmasūtras

Adhyāsa-bhāṣyam with Catussūtri [The first four sūtras] with Śaṅkarabhāṣyam and the gloss, Ratnaprabhā

Prakaraṇa Granthas

Tattvabodha of Śri Ādi Śaṅkarācārya

Pañcadasī of Śri Vidyāranya [1-6 Chapters]

Sādhanā Pañcakam of Śri Ādi Śaṅkarācārya

Vedāntasāra of sadānanda

Vivekacūdāmaṇi [Selected verses] of Śri Ādi Śaṅkarācārya

Maniṣāpañcakam of Śri Ādi Śaṅkarācārya

Miscellaneous

Other schools of Indian Philosophy

General Introduction to the Vedas and Vedic Ritual

Guided Meditation [500 hours]

April 15, 2016

Brahmaprakasananda

Chief Acharya

Vedanta Syllabus

Dr. Shrikant Jichkar Memorial

ARSHA VIJNANA GURUKULAM

Vedapuri, Nagpur

This is to certify that **Ashwini Kumar Aggarwal** has received instruction in SANSKRIT as detailed below during the THREE YEAR RESIDENTIAL COURSE IN VEDANTA AND SANSKRIT, which commenced on January 15, 2013.

[Approximately 1000 Hours of Instruction]

General

A Sanskrit Manual for High Schools, Part I by R.Antoine S.J.
Second Book of Sanskrit by R.G.Bhandarkar
Teach Yourself Sanskrit [Saṁskṛtasvādhyāyaḥ]

— Prathamā Dīkṣā of Rāṣṭriya Saṁskṛta Saṁsthānam

Varṇamālā — Alphabets

Sambhāṣaṇam — Conversation

Vākyavyavahāraḥ — Sentence Construction

Vākyavistaraḥ — Advanced Sentence Construction

Pariśiṣṭam — Miscellaneous

— Dvitīya Dīkṣā of Rāṣṭriya Saṁskṛta Saṁsthānam

Vyavārapradīpaḥ

Sṛṣṭi — Rachna Sagar Books 1,2,3,6,7,8

Bāla Rāmāyaṇam — R.S.Vadyar

Reader I — R.S.Vadyar

The Aṣṭādhyāyī of Pāṇini

Pāṇinīya-vyākaraṇam was taught by the method of Siddhānta Kaumudī with its commentaries along with Kāśikā Vṛtti, with its commentaries, to give the pūrvāpara connections. The following sections were covered:

Samjñāprakaraṇam	Sārvadhātuka-lakāras of the daśa gaṇas	Paribhāṣāprakaraṇam
Ārdhadhātuka-lakāras	Pañcasandhiprakaraṇam	Nyantaprakriyā
Subantaprakaraṇam	Sannantaprakriyā	Samāsaprakaraṇam
Yañantaprakriyā	Samāsāntaprakaraṇam	Yaṅlugantaprakriyā
Taddhitaprakaraṇam	Nāmadhātuprakaraṇam	Stripratyayaprakaraṇam
Kaṇḍvādiprakaraṇam	Avyayaprakaraṇam	Pratyayamālāprakaraṇam
Kārakaprakaraṇam	Ātmanepadaprakriyā	Kṛdantaprakaraṇam
Parasmaipadaprakriyā	Pūrvakṛdantaprakaraṇam	Bhāvakarmaprakriyā
Unādiprakaraṇam	Karmakartṛprakriyā	Uttarakṛdantaprakaraṇam
Lakārārthaprakriyā	Tiṅantaprakaraṇam	

Miscellaneous

Chanting [300 hours]
Vedic Chanting, Bhāṣya Pārāyaṇam, Stotras, Aṣṭottaras, Sahasranāmas and Bhajans
Introduction to Classical Music [20 hours]
Introduction to Āgama Śāstras [2 hours]

Brahmaprakasananda

April 15, 2016

Chief Acharya

Sanskrit Syllabus

Arsha Vijnana Gurukulam AVG Nagpur

The Gurukul is an institute for the study of Indian Philosophy, Culture, Sanskrit and Yoga. It was founded by Pujya Swami Dayananda Saraswati[1] and Dr. Shrikant Jichkar[2]. Its president is Rajashri Jichkar[3] and chief acharya is Swamini Brahmaprakasananda Saraswati[4].

Website https://avgnagpur.org/
Email: online.avg.nagpur@gmail.com
Google Maps code: 6Q72+49 Bazargaon, Maharashtra

Phone +91 98902 93641 (Swapnil Jatkar, Admin)
Arsha Vijnana Gurukulam, Vedapuri
Dorli-Bazargaon Road, Post-Raulgaon, Tahsil Katol
Nagpur 441502 Maharashtra Bhārat.

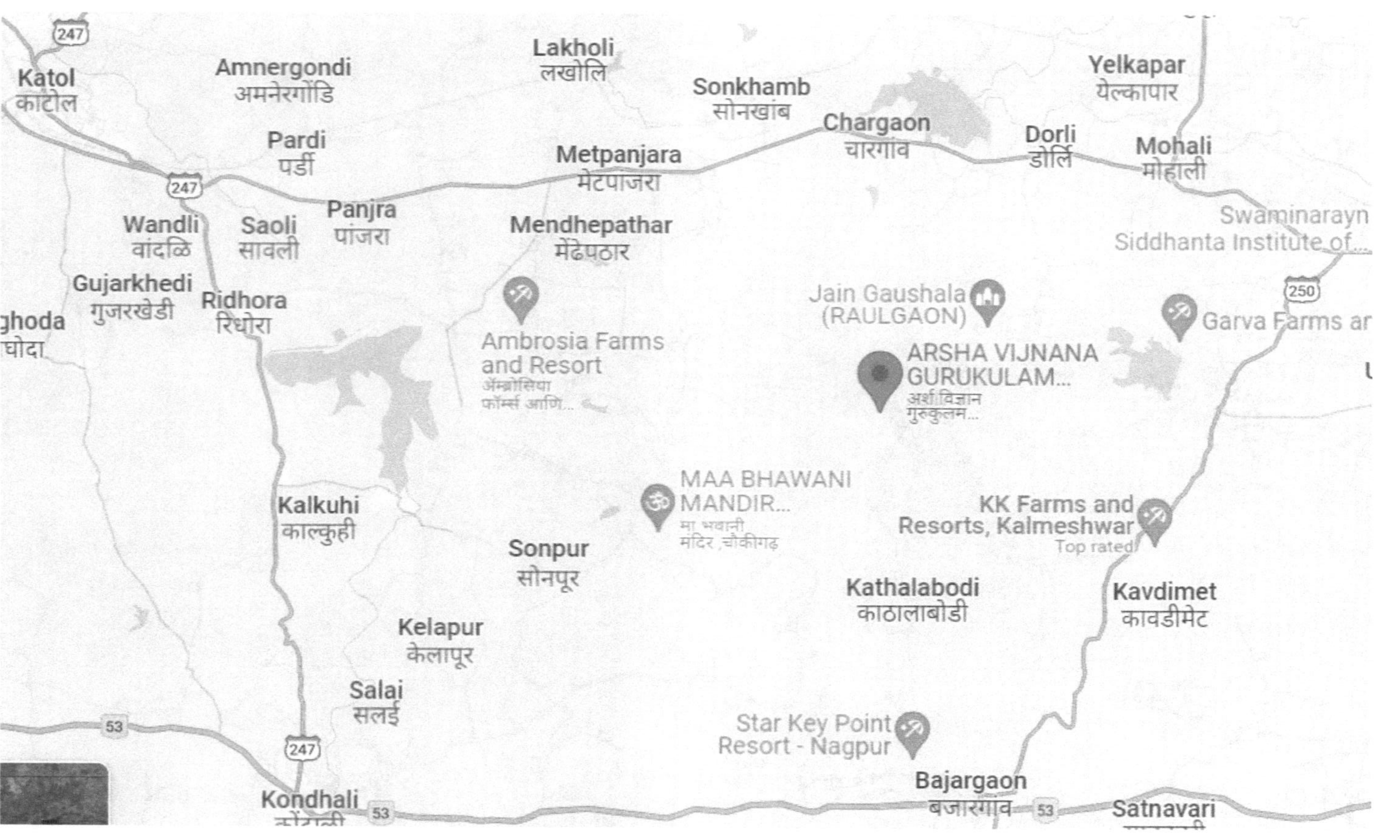

Courtesy Google Maps. AVG Nagpur

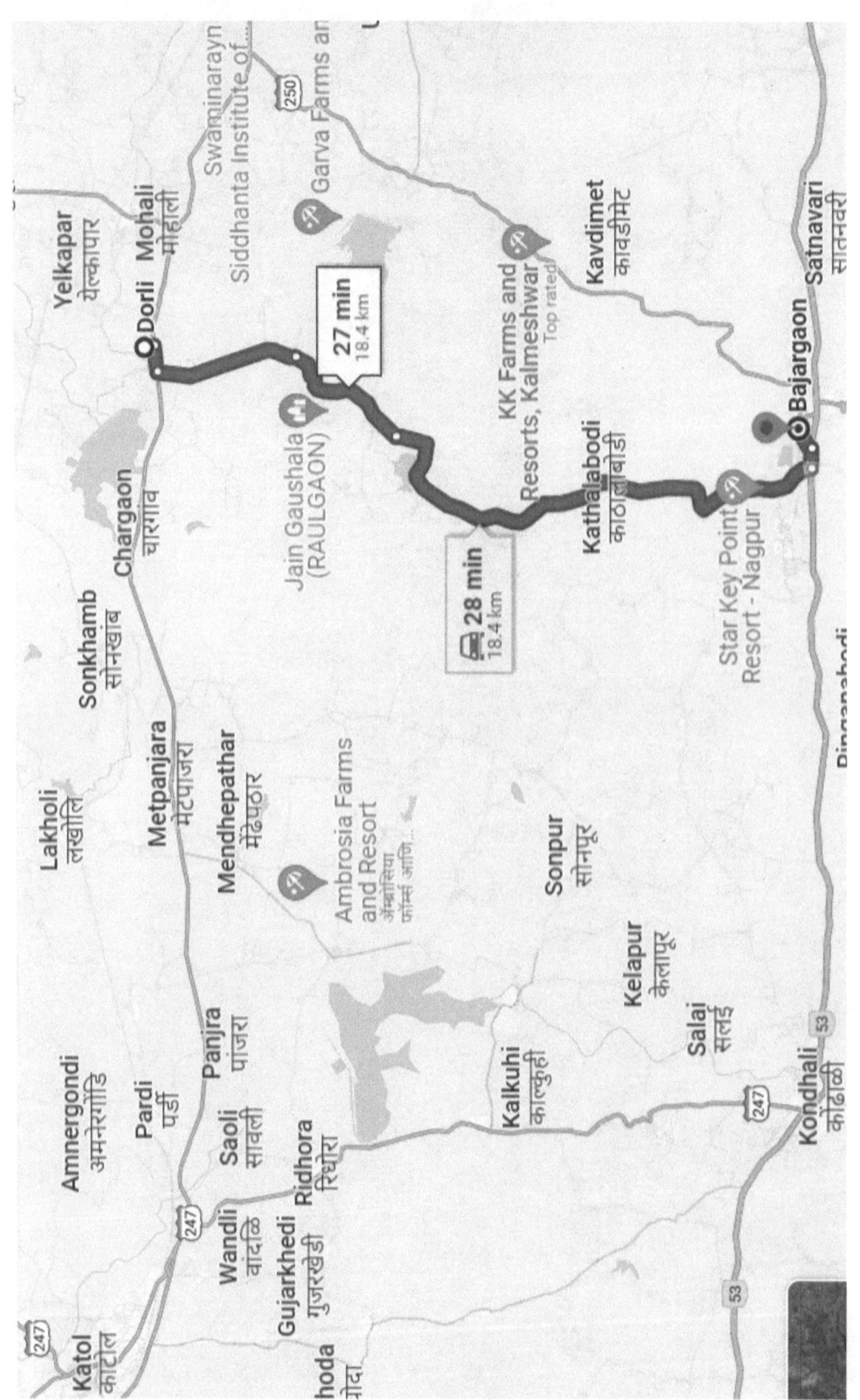

Courtesy Google Maps. Dorli to Bazargaon Road via Gurukul.

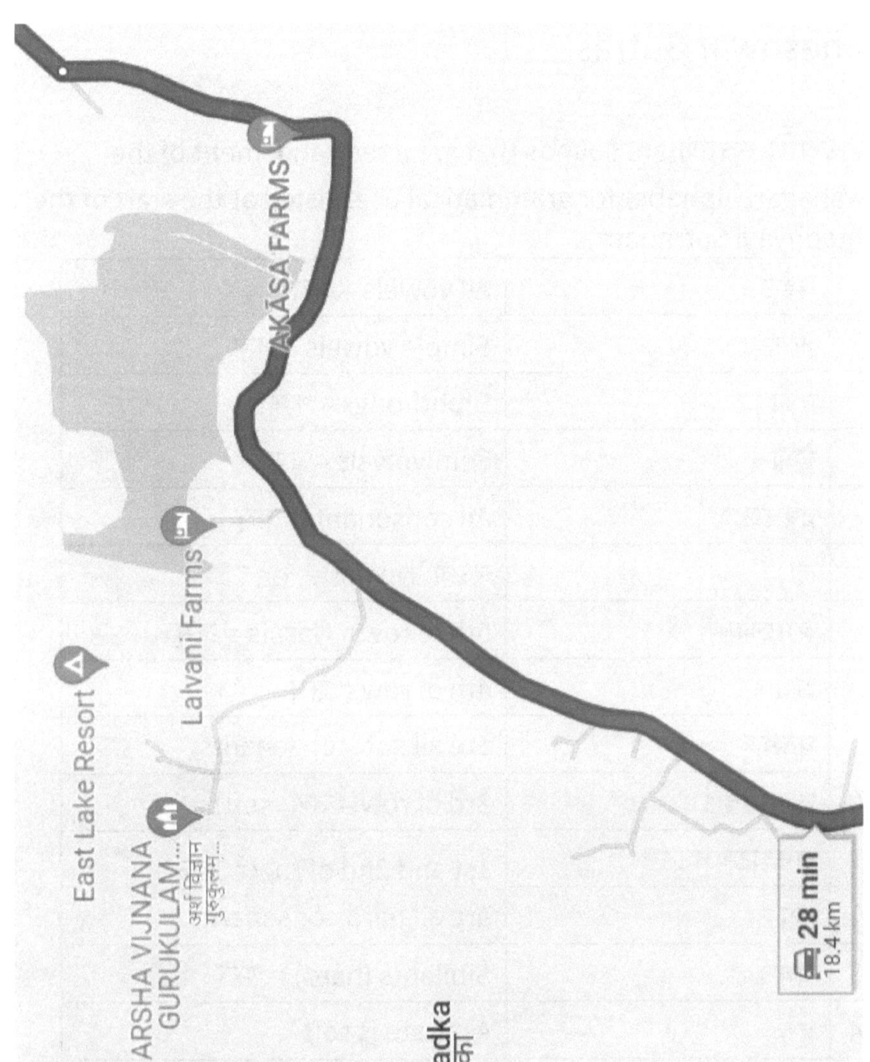

Courtesy Google Maps. Gurukul and Lake.

Maheshwar Sutras

माहेश्वराणि सूत्राणि are sounds that are a rearrangement of the Devanagari Alphabet for grammatical use. Listed at the start of the Ashtadhyayi Sutrapatha.

1	अइउण्	All vowels = अच्
2	ऋऌक्	Simple vowels = अक्
3	एओङ्	Diphthongs = एच्
4	ऐऔच्	Semivowels = यण्
5	हयवरट्	All consonants = हल्
6	लँण्	ल्+अँ, No nasal for र्
7	अमङणनम्	5th of row = Nasals = अम्
8	झभञ्	4th of row = झष्
9	घढधष्	are all soft consonants
10	जबगडदश्	3rd of row = जश् (soft)
11	खफछठथचटतव्	1st and 2nd of row = खय्
12	कपय्	are all hard consonants
13	शषसर्	Sibilants (hard) = शर्
14	हल्	Aspirate is soft

Consonants have been written with अकार solely for enunciation. But the लँण् = ल् अँ ण् contains लकार, anunasika Tag अँ, and a consonant Tag ण् ।

Pratyaharas

SN	Maheshwar Sutras	Pratyaharas	Count
1	अइउण्	अण्	1
2	ऋऌक्	अक् इक् उक्	3
3	एओङ्	एङ्	1
4	ऐऔच्	अच् इच् एच् ऐच्	4
5	हयवरट्	अट्	1
6	लँण्	अण् इण् यण् ⁢रँ	3
7	ञमङणनम्	अम् यम् ङम् ⁢अम्	3
8	झभञ्	यञ्	1
9	घढधष्	झष् भष्	2
10	जबगडदश्	अश् हश् वश् झश् जश् बश्	6
11	खफछठथँचटतव्	छव् ⁢खँ	1
12	कपय्	यय् मय् झय् खय् ⁢चय् अय्	4
13	शषसर्	यर् झर् खर् चर् शर्	5
14	हल्	अल् हल् वल् रल् झल् शल्	6
		Basic Count of Pratyaharas =	41
	Extended Count 41 + 3 = 44 + 2 with later grammarians =		46

Epilogue

Vedanta and Sanskrit are a rare combination of that hallowed knowledge, that may very well turn our planet and this enormous creation into our best friend.

सर्वे भवन्तु सुखिनः । सर्वे सन्तु निरामयाः ।

सर्वे भद्राणि पश्यन्तु । मा कश्चिद् दुःख भाग् भवेत् ॥

ॐ शान्तिः शान्तिः शान्तिः ॥

When faith has blossomed in life, Every step is led by the Divine.

Sri Sri Ravi Shankar

Om Namah Shivaya

जय गुरुदेव

www.ingramcontent.com/pod-product-compliance
Lightning Source LLC
Chambersburg PA
CBHW021009180726
47993CB00019B/2129